Brad

Her.

trips we took throughout
Asia, and those amazing
days living in Singapore
Thanks for sharing your
Adventures — Mike

The Millennial's Guide to Business Travel

Lessons for the Next Generation of Road Warriors

Safe Travels!

Michael Puldy

Michael L Puldy

The Millennial's Guide to Business Travel
by Michael L Puldy

Cover Photo: Michael L Puldy
Contributors: Brandi Boatner, Andrew Burger, Michele Puldy Burger, Tali Burger, Cathy Band, Pat Corcoran, Brad Donaldson, Erich Elit, Michael Errity, Jess Gardner, Steve Gilbert, Michael Goldman, William Hahn, Scott Jones, Ian Mac Quarrie, Chris Pantano, Don Platt, Michele Kochoff Platt, Adrienne Hahn Puldy, Carol Puldy, Nathaniel Puldy, Stephen Puldy, Susan Schreitmueller, Amy Turkel, and Susan Weiss

Edited by: Rae DeVito and Charlotte Errity

First Printed Edition
ISBN-10: 1-537-13088-9
ISBN-13: 978-1-537-13088-0

First eBook Edition
ISBN-10 0-692-75517-9
ISBN-13 978-0-692-75517-4

Printed by CreateSpace
Available on Kindle and other devices

FOR EVERY SITUATION. THIS WORK IS SOLD WITH THE UNDERSTANDING THAT THE AUTHOR IS NOT ENGAGED IN RENDERING LEGAL, ACCOUNTING, OR OTHER PROFESSIONAL SERVICES. IF PROFESSIONAL ASSISTANCE IS REQUIRED, THE SERVICES OF A COMPETENT PROFESSIONAL PERSON SHOULD BE SOUGHT. THE AUTHOR SHALL NOT BE LIABLE FOR DAMAGES ARISING HEREFROM. THE FACT THAT AN ORGANIZATION OR WEBSITE IS REFERRED TO IN THIS WORK AS A CITATION AND/OR A POTENTIAL SOURCE OF FURTHER INFORMATION DOES NOT MEAN THAT THE AUTHOR ENDORSES THE INFORMATION THE ORGANIZATION OR WEBSITE MAY PROVIDE OR RECOMMENDATIONS IT MAY MAKE. FURTHER, READERS SHOULD BE AWARE THAT INTERNET WEBSITES LISTED IN THIS WORK MAY HAVE CHANGED OR DISAPPEARED BETWEEN WHEN THIS WORK WAS WRITTEN AND WHEN IT IS READ.

For those interested in more information browse www.nextgentraveler.com or send an email to: questions@nextgentraveler.com

To Zachary, Alexander and Nathaniel

Preface

Are you new to the world of business travel? If so, welcome to my world!

I LOVE to travel! Ever since my first airplane flight from Jacksonville, Florida to Miami, I've always wanted a traveling job. Over my life, I've flown over 2.8 million air miles, covering six continents, and spent thousands of nights in hotel rooms. For more than a decade, I've regularly obtained what's called a "1K" elite membership on United Airlines which means I fly over 100,000 miles a year, and I'm in the top 1% of their annual client base.[1] Looking across the thirty airlines I've flown, the airlines at the top of my most flown list includes: United Airlines (1.3 million miles), Delta Airlines (700,000 miles) and American Airlines (600,000 miles).

To put those miles into perspective, over my life, I have flown the equivalent of circling the planet 112 times or five round trips to the moon. In terms of time, assuming the average air speed for all those miles equaled 475 miles per hour, I've spent almost 5,900 hours or eight-plus months of my life sitting inside an airplane.[2] Fun facts!

I'm also a Diamond VIP at Hilton, a Platinum member at Hyatt, and a Gold member at Marriott and Sheraton. Having these nice jewels tied to my name at hotel check-in, as you will discover, is very important.

Through all this travel, I've shared tips with my children, our friends, and total strangers. Today, my three boys are starting their own travel experiences, and I realize there's an entire new generation of business travelers taking to the skies and to the roads. A new generation of road warriors has begun their quest to grow business, make money and have some fun along the way.

---

[1] United Airlines doesn't publish a breakdown of its members at each award level so the statistic that United 1Ks are the top one percent of United Airlines' frequent fliers is educated speculation

[2] For inquiring minds, the farthest distance from the Earth to the Moon is 252,088 miles (405,696 km), and the circumference of the Earth is roughly 24,901 miles (40,075 km).

If you are part of this elite set of millennials, or just starting a life of business travel, this book is for you. A business trip can be as fun as it is productive with the right planning and the right understanding of the problems and the challenges you might face.

This book outlines ways to maximize your time in first class, be awarded the car upgrade and explains how to almost always enjoy the larger and nicer hotel room.

Learn options to bypass those long lines at security, at immigration and never wait for your bag.

In addition to learning over a hundred different travel tips, read true-life stories from fellow domestic and international road warriors about their strange and unexpected experiences as they traveled from one business destination to another.

And, I've enlisted a close friend, and an ultra-experienced world business traveler, Susan Schreitmueller, to add her perspective. Susan is technologist, and she is a distinguished engineer, which means Susan is incredibly smart, resourceful, and successful; and, yes, she is also very well-traveled. Susan has traveled over 4.3 million air miles across six continents, and spent her expat days living in Dubai, U.A.E. Throughout the book, you will see a sidebar called "A Woman's Perspective." These are Susan's comments relevant to the chapter.

Becoming a road warrior isn't easy, but the life experiences are priceless. Now, pack your bag, suit up, and let's go!

I've traveled over one million miles on American Airlines, one million miles on Delta Airlines, and 300,000 miles on Emirates. That's a *LOT* of experiences, both good and bad. I've also traveled through some VERY dicey areas, so I might err on the side of caution when it comes to safety and my "backup plan." I will also tell you, like it or not, a woman has some safety considerations above what a man might consider. I found this book to be interesting, valuable AND entertaining – So enjoy your read!

A Woman's Perspective by Susan Schreitmueller

Chapter 1: Introduction

Welcome to the world of business travel! Many people travel for business. In fact, business travel makes up one-third of all travel according to the U.S. Travel Association. In 2015, U.S. business travel accounted for $296 billion out of $947 billion spent on both business and leisure travel.[3]

According to the same study, business travel also generates around $48 billion in tax revenue and over 2.4 million jobs. Needless to say, business travel is big business on its own. There are many different airlines, hotels, rental car agencies, restaurants, credit card companies and others trying to win your business.

However, business travel is very different than personal travel. Most importantly, your time is not your own. Your company is not paying you to go to New York City to see a show on Broadway or to finance your dinner at Per Se. Your company wants you to fly to New York City, stay in a relatively inexpensive but safe hotel, eat dinner while you work, and return back to your home desk within hours of concluding your business meeting.

Large corporations have per diem rates for food, pre-negotiated rates for hotels, preferred car rental agencies, and preferred airlines. If you violate their travel rules, you could be fired. On the other hand, while smaller companies have fewer rules governing travel policies, they are equally concerned about travel spending.

The purpose of this guide is to help you make the best choices associated with your business travel that conforms to your company policies, but also allows you to optimize your time away from home. You'll learn tips to minimize the time you spend sitting in the last row of the airplane watching people go to the lavatory; you'll read strategies on how to avoid staying

---

[3] www.USTravel.org See the **U.S. Travel Answer Sheet** which outlines facts about the U.S. travel industry.

in a hotel located in a demilitarized zone; and you'll have options to steer you away from a 2:00 a.m. dinner at Waffle House. Don't get me wrong, if you travel enough you will have these moments, but they should be the few and not the norm.

The majority of this book is focused on domestic travel, and specifically domestic travel within the United States. However, no book on business travel would be complete without some concentration on international travel. Chapter 13 is all about traveling across borders.

While international travel can be the most rewarding experience of your entire life, international travel can also turn into the most unpredictable and harrowing of your life experiences. Imagine being stuck on the tarmac of a remote airport in a foreign country where no one speaks your language, there's no mobile phone service, and you are a hundred miles from any place remotely resembling a modern city.

Travel stories are the best stories.

Chapter 2: The Beginning of Your Adventure

Monday morning. Your boss calls you into their office and asks if you can be in Chicago for a Wednesday morning meeting. Can you?

Of course, you say, "YES!" If you're lucky, your boss gives you a contact name in Chicago with a meeting address. Is your meeting downtown or in Schaumburg? Both considered Chicago, but each will give you a different business travel experience.

Regardless, the clock is ticking. You need to perform your day job, figure out your travel logistics, prep for your business meeting, and be in Chicago in less than 48 hours. Start by focusing on the travel mechanics.

Business Travel Policies

If you work for a small or privately held company, most likely there are no travel policies so you are blazing a new trail. If you work for a Global 2000 company, then expect a small book detailing travel rules. In this case, read the manual, and then read it again. You want to be an astute student of your company's travel game plan because violating these rules is the easiest way to be fired.

Extremely large companies have business controls organizations and corporate auditors who spend their entire working day looking for travel violations. It's easy for them to find red flags because the rules are both robust and complicated; therefore, it's easy for employees to make mistakes.

If you are a founder of a startup, then you have to decide how footloose you want to be with your company's travel. Is first class travel acceptable? Do you want to set one standard as a perk for your executive team and another for your staff? Do you just want to accept the cheapest form of travel? Remember choosing the lowest price airfare or the cheapest hotel room may not be the lowest cost when you look at the big picture.

The Corporate Credit Card

When traveling on business make sure you have a corporate credit card. Most companies issue a corporate American Express or a corporate Visa. Regardless of which card your company issues, I find it is best to travel with both an American Express and a Visa or a MasterCard. My corporate card is an American Express and I always take a personal Visa just in case my American Express isn't accepted. In the U.S., it's rare American Express isn't accepted, but it happens. Internationally, American Express is accepted in almost every hotel and with every airline, but again your experience will vary greatly for restaurants, metros, taxis, and ATMs.

Travel Tip: Constantly think about your backup plan, and in the case of credit cards, always travel with two types. It's rare that a place of business doesn't take two or three different types of credit cards, but there's always the exception including those places that only take cash. As long as you carry multiple kinds of credit cards, and a decent amount of cash, you'll rarely have a problem conducting a financial transaction.

Be careful about using your personal card for travel, and always use your corporate credit card for business transactions. Even though you are personally responsible for the expenses placed on your corporate credit card, the corporate card allows for your business charges to be easily called out.

When you use your personal card for business travel expenses, your company may not reimburse you, take a lengthy amount of time to reimburse you, or may even consider your expenses questionable.

Worst case scenario: if your company goes into bankruptcy and your charges are on your personal card, you may never be reimbursed.

Moreover, be sensitive to credit card fraud. Credit card fraud has become more rampant than ever, and I find it common to replace several credit cards every year because of fraudulent charges. Even when you are not traveling, regularly check your credit card's online system to confirm your account has not been compromised. And, as a proactive measure, don't hesitate to contact your credit card company semi-annually, or annually, and just request a new card.

I applaud carrying at least one other personal credit card, spare cash and an ATM card (preapproved for international travel) to withdraw cash. I also keep emergency cash in a totally separate and hidden location in my suitcase or carry-on. Read my travel story at the end of Chapter 4 and you'll see why!

A Woman's Perspective

Travel Websites

If your company has a corporate travel website, that website is typically focused on company policies, approved hotels, and other important things to know when on the road for the company.

The reality is you want to have your "go to" websites and travel apps with you at all times. Besides the standard airline, hotel, and rental car apps, here are some of my favorite travel apps:

Name	Description	Comments
Currency	Currency exchange rates	www.xe.com International exchange rates
Expedia	Flight and Hotel Booking System	www.expedia.com
Flight View	Real-time flight tracker and airport delay tracker	www.flightview.com
Google Maps	Navigation	www.google.com/maps
International SOS	Medical and travel security assistance	www.internationalsos.com Requires corporate plan
Kayak	Flight and hotel booking system	www.kayak.com
Local Eats	Local favorites for dining	www.localeats.com
Open Table	Restaurant reservations	www.opentable.com
Smart Traveler	U.S. Department of State notification system	step.state.gov/step/ Sometimes it's a good idea to have the U.S. government know your whereabouts
TripAdvisor	Ratings for everything	www.tripadvisor.com

Uber	Car taxi service	www.uber.com
UrbanDaddy	Entertainment guide	www.urbandaddy.com Quirky way to find things to do
Waze	Efficient navigation	www.waze.com
Weather	Weather guidance	www.weather.com
Worldmate	Trip consolidator	www.worldmate.com All your trip details consolidated
Yelp	Ratings for everything	www.yelp.com

Nightlife

Even though you're going on a business trip, remember to have fun, find a way to explore the area, and try to experience some of the local nightlife. If you're visiting a large metropolitan city, you'll typically enjoy lots of choices, while staying in smaller towns may mean fewer options. Whether you are visiting a large city or a small remote location, do a little bit of research before you go.

TripAdvisor and Yelp are two great places to start. You can find interesting attractions and fun places to eat. Also, perform a Google search for the local entertainment magazine like **LA Weekly** in Los Angeles, **SF Weekly** in San Francisco, **WestWorld** in Denver and **The Village Voice** in New York. The **TimeOut** online magazine is also a good source of entertainment information covering dozens of cities around the globe.

Also, if you think you'll have some extra time in the city you're visiting, or you're uncertain of your agenda, check out **GroupOn** or **LikeALocalGuide**. GroupOn provides a great way to stretch your food budget while LikeALocalGuide provides local tips on places to go and things to see.

Regardless, research your destination before you travel and upon arrival. Every now and then you can find great music, a favorite sporting event, theater, or perhaps a comedian in town the same day you are there.

You just never know what might happen; going out for the night, whether it is table for one at a trendy restaurant, or enjoying a beer at a local sport bar, is always more fun than sitting in your hotel room watching cable or staring at Facebook. Even sitting in a local coffee shop with your laptop can be surprisingly uplifting.

Cops have an expression (yes – I was a cop for a short while): nothing good happens after 2:00 a.m. As a woman, I am particularly sensitive to remaining "situationally aware" when out on the streets after dark. Limit your use of a cell phone and be aware of the part of town you are in. Arrange to call a colleague upon arrival back at your hotel, or at a pre-arranged time, and let them know where you plan to go. Ladies – you also want to be aware that you might become more famous than you'd like when someone posts your good time on Facebook. Remember, even if you are harmlessly out with a bunch of your married colleagues, it's a good idea to remain – SITUATIONALLY AWARE.

A Woman's Perspective

Travel Story: Business Trip Pregame, Courtesy of Scott Jones, Texas

When I was in my twenties, the night before one of my business trips, my very bright roommate, who I also worked with, talked me into going drinking.

He told me the morning trip would be a piece of cake, and that I should go out with him and his rugby buddies. After a long night of partying, I barely made the train, smelled like booze when I connected later that morning with my boss, and was nervous all day in front of the client. It took me three months of being a good boy in the office before they let me travel on another business trip. I have never traveled unprepared again.

Chapter 3: Pack Your Bags

If there was ever a prime example of the phrase, "Pictures speak louder than words," the 1971 American Tourister Gorilla commercial is it! This commercial set the standard for how luggage needs to be both rugged and look good. In the commercial, luggage is given to a gorilla, a metaphor for all types of luggage handlers. The gorilla then proceeds to beat the daylights out of the luggage. American Tourister's tagline said it all, "It's not how good it looks, it's how long it looks good!"[4] American Tourister is still in business today, but doesn't have the cache of the 70s and the 80s.

Regardless, choosing your travel bag and efficiently packing it could be one of the biggest challenges of your entire adventure. I hear stories of people taking hours to pack for a trip. Some people pack the night before while others pack the day of travel. My favorite are the people who pack literally minutes before they are supposed to head to the airport.

Nevertheless, packing is an art.

The fundamental theme incorporates costume changes, location climate, how many nights you expect to be on the road, and the size of the suitcase you are packing.

Are you away for one night and headed to a warm part of the world? Or, are you traveling for multiple days during the winter heading first to New York and then down to Miami Beach before heading home? You need a coat for New York, while just a light jacket or sweater for Miami Beach.

But before you pack, pick the right luggage.

---

[4] 1971 American Tourister "Gorilla" Commercial, and 1980 Gorilla vs Luggage https://goo.gl/eDkdGQ

Here's a good strategy: lighter is better. Pack, and take half out; come back an hour later and take another half out! I find a spreadsheet works wonders when I'm looking at options for two - five days of travel. Pick a neutral color for a skirt, pants or a suit, rotate tops, and always pack one nice blouse or one dress for going out. Also, don't underestimate the versatility of a good blazer across a multi-day and multi-location trip. Do pack a spare set of shoes, but try to limit yourself to two plus maybe a pair of workout shoes. (I like Vibrams.) When I pack to go home, I roll my clothes to create more room. A Ziploc bag with the air sucked out does wonders if I am tight on space. As a side note, I pack a couple of extra gallon size Ziploc bags for wet suits or items I wash out before I check out of the hotel.

A Woman's Perspective

The Luggage

If you're right out of school, chances are you are still traveling with your college backpack or soft-shell duffel. At some point you need respectable luggage and the options are plentiful.

When taking that first big step and buying a serious piece of luggage, pick something that rolls, fits easily in a plane's overhead bin, and can expand a few inches so you can bring more stuff home than you brought. That means something 22" long by 14" wide by 9" deep or thereabouts, and it must have wheels. Either two wheels so it's easy to drag your bag, or for someone who likes to push or walk alongside a bag, look for a four-wheeled suitcase.

After traveling for twenty-five years, I finally broke down and bought a Tumi carry-on bag. I couldn't believe I spent so much money for luggage, but it was totally worth the expense. Now I have six different Tumi bags, and I always ask myself why I waited so long to buy a major league piece of luggage.

The key message is buy something that's durable, has a warranty (Tumi has a five-year warranty while competitors like Briggs and Riley offer a lifetime warranty), and easy to repair when you have a problem. It's also important to think about the purpose of your bag. Will you check it? Will you need to expand it to support multiple travel days? Two-wheels? Four-wheels? No wheels? Does the retractable handle seem flimsy and could it break? Does your bag have outside pockets for quick access items like magazines and power chargers, and will you have any issues lifting this fully loaded bag into an overhead baggage bin?

Even if you aren't ready to spend $600 for a piece of luggage, you too can be a "baller on a budget" if you do your research and shop wisely for a quality bag at a bargain price.[5]

One time, I bought a 24-inch long bag for my carry-on. I was told this was an "international" length. The problem was most of the planes I flew had domestic configurations so there was a 50/50 chance the bag would not fit in the overhead bin; moreover, on many occasions the gate agent would express a concern the bag was too long. In those instances, I would socially engineer, or hack my way past the agent by declaring, "the bag always fits," and "I'm a 1K, and I never have a problem." Most of the time, that worked, but now I rarely use that bag unless I'm checking it.

Regardless, while I was often successful talking my slightly lengthy bag on the plane, it's not uncommon to see travelers get rejected. Either at the gate while being forced to ram their oversized back into a metal bag template, or worse, while

---

[5] Great luggage can also be found at various mass-market retailers like Marshalls, TJ Maxx, and many online stores.

fighting with the flight attendant – on the plane – as they try to jam their bag into an overhead bin.

Don't make my mistake! Buy a bag and bring a bag that always fits on the plane.

In 2013, Marc Weber Tobias wrote a great article in **Forbes** that is as applicable today as it was then. *How to Choose Luggage for Business Travel*[6] covers many of the same points I mentioned, but goes into more detail on luggage selection criteria.

In the end, you need to make your own decision on brand, size and function and, of course, price – likely the biggest factor. Consider your luggage your first big investment in becoming a road warrior. If you plan to cover thousands of miles every month, and spend a noticeable part of your life in hotel rooms, spend the extra money and find a quality bag that's "bullet proof." Remember, while you may only be flying to Chicago, your bag may fly to Australia, Germany, and London before rendezvousing with you in Chicago.

> **Travel Tip: Never place your laptop or your tablet in your luggage.** This may seem like a tip from Captain Obvious, but I continually hear stories about computers being smashed, or worse, stolen because someone was lazy, placed it in their luggage, and then had to check their bag at the last minute while boarding an airplane. Remember, especially when flying small commuter planes, no matter how small your luggage, you may be forced to check your bag.

---

[6] Tobias, Marc Weber, **Forbes**, *How to Choose Luggage for Business Travel*, July 9, 2013

> Check a bag's weight when UNPACKED. Lighter is better, but remember your bag may very well have over 1,000 pounds of luggage stacked on top of it. Keep bag strength in mind when packing breakables!
>
> A Woman's Perspective

The Personal Carry-on

Let's be clear, your luggage is for your clothes and the things you can replace or live without while your personal carry-on contains your life's nuclear launch codes. You cannot afford to lose this bag – EVER!

This bag goes under-the-seat in front of you on the airplane and stays with you in the backseat of the Uber. This bag is always within eyeshot at your business meeting, and slides under the table at your business dinner. There are times you must check your luggage no matter how small, but you will never check this personal carry-on.

Women have additional options and challenges when choosing an under the seat personal carry-on. Some women bring a purse and insert it in their carry-on prior to boarding so they conform to the airline's one bag and one personal item carry-on limit. Others change out their purse and put all personal items into a single bag that fits under the seat. Bag options include a Longchamp large Le Pliage tote, a Briggs and Riley Baseline Tote, or a Louis Vuitton Neverfull. These large bags fit computers, chargers and headphones plus personal items like cosmetics and keys so you don't have to reach into the overhead bin during the flight.

Regardless, when you're on the road, the personal carry-on bag is your lifeline to the world. Your computer, tablet, keys, jewelry, glasses, access cards, power cords, emergency battery, headphones, printed flight plans, hotel confirmation codes, emergency food, medications, and more is contained within this bag. For the true road warrior, this bag allows your office to exist wherever you want it to be. It's important to be fully self-sufficient on the road, and this bag and its contents make it possible.

I can't describe the number of times I've been saved by having this bag with me because I'm able to set up my portable office anywhere on the planet. I even carry a portable hotspot for those rare conditions where wireless isn't accessible.

Here's an unabridged list of what goes into my personal carry-on:

- ✓ Apple EarPods
- ✓ Apple iPad for business and iPad for personal (yes, two)
- ✓ Apple iPhone for business and iPhone for personal
- ✓ Apple iPod with my entire music library of 27,568 songs
- ✓ Apple MacBook 60W power charger
- ✓ Apple MacBook Air with Case Logic cover
- ✓ Assorted toiletries (for international travel only)
- ✓ Assorted travel clothes (for international travel only)
- ✓ Bose QuietComfort wireless noise cancelling headphones
- ✓ Bose Soundtrue Ultra-in-ear headphones
- ✓ Bottled water
- ✓ Business cards
- ✓ Electrical power converters (for international travel only)
- ✓ Emergency U.S. currency
- ✓ Eye drops
- ✓ Eyeshades
- ✓ Folder containing important travel and business papers
- ✓ Key chain with assorted house and car keys
- ✓ LG Tone Pro Bluetooth headset
- ✓ Moleskin notepad
- ✓ Multiple USB memory sticks
- ✓ Reading glasses
- ✓ Sunglasses with case
- ✓ Tissues or napkins
- ✓ Travel food
- ✓ Tumi accessory pouch containing chargers and cables
- ✓ Two pens
- ✓ Wallet filled with loyalty and frequent flier cards
- ✓ Yellow highlighter

I know this seems like a lot of stuff and some of these items are probably questionable, but the more you travel the more you experience problems you never anticipated which makes all this stuff relevant.

As an example, there was a time I only traveled with my standard earphones, but then I bought Bose noise cancelling headphones for the plane and Bose in-ear headphones for times when not flying. Once, I left my in-ear headphones at home. Normally, not having my in-ear headphones is no big deal, but then I was faced with a seven-hour delay in the Raleigh-Durham airport. It was awkward listening to music on my Bose headphones while wandering the airport, so I shopped for a low cost, temporary option. Needless to say, the replacement pair I found was both poor quality and crazy expensive. Now, I keep an inexpensive pair of Apple EarPods at the bottom of my bag to be opened in case of emergency.

Another example from my list is the emergency U.S. currency.

A friend from Australia gave me this suggestion. He told me there are times when ATM's don't work or you don't have enough cash to travel. Since everyone accepts U.S. currency, he suggested I carry $100 all the time.

I now keep a c-note buried in my bag. Fortunately, I've never had to use it, but there's always a first time, and I consider my hidden money cheap travel insurance.[7]

See the pattern?

Packing for travel is all about preparing for contingencies. Ask yourself, "What's your backup plan?"

Here's another example, for men, pack extra collar stays for your dress shirts. Why? Try looking for collar stays at 10:35 p.m. at the hotel gift shop.

---

[7] A C-note is slang for a $100 bill. C stands for "centum" the Latin word for 100, and U.S. paper currency has the word "note" written on the bill.

> As a woman, I carry at least three Band-Aids, of which one has pre-applied antibiotic for shoe blisters. I also pack various sized safety pins for emergencies, and yes, I've used safety pins a bunch of times for wardrobe malfunctions. In addition, I never travel without Advil or aspirin, and a set of soft ear plugs in my carry-on. For colds and flu, I stick with my cold tablet of choice, and if I'm traveling internationally, I carry Cipro. Moreover, if you have any prescription medications in your carry-on, make sure you have the printed Rx.
>
> A Woman's Perspective

The Bathroom Essentials

Unless you've never been on a plane before, you know all liquids in your carry-on must fit in one quart-sized bag. The TSA liquid policy is simple.[8] If you plan to bring liquids through the TSA security checkpoint, and on the plane, no container can exceed 3.4 ounces (100 milliliters), and all liquids must fit in a single one quart-sized bag. One bag per traveler! The exemptions are medications and infant and child nourishments. If you can't comply with this mandate, then you must pack your liquids inside a checked bag.

In reference to the type of bag for your liquids, I went through dozens of plastic Ziploc bags before I found a stronger and eco-friendly way. Now, I use a Sephora "Beauty on the Fly"

---

[8] www.tsa.gov/travel/security-screening/liquids-rule

TSA-friendly travel bag found for $4.95. My bag is five-years-old, has traveled roughly 600,000 air miles, and still works for me today.

> **Travel Tip: Keep a stocked bag of toiletries exclusively for business travel.** While keeping a full second set of cosmetics may not be practical, the majority of the bathroom stuff you need for a business trip is simple and easily affordable. Moreover, no longer packing and unpacking a sundry bag before each trip will give you peace of mind that you haven't forgotten anything. Scouring your house for a razor, a toothbrush, a three-ounce container of toothpaste, and floss as you pack will be a thing of the past.

As far as finding good sundry supplies, many grocery stores and pharmacies sell travel-sized products that easily conform to the TSA liquid guidelines. For this reason, I never take a large bottle of shaving cream or a twelve-ounce tube of toothpaste on a business trip. Since they don't conform to the TSA liquid standards, I would constantly be checking my bag. Plus, the larger containers consume precious cargo space and add unnecessary weight.

I typically stock up on travel size items during my regular grocery trips and maintain a small at-home inventory of shaving cream, toothpaste, and mouthwash. This allows me to easily restock my travel bag upon returning from the current trip, so I'm always ready for the next one.

Personally, I love reusable tubes like goToobs, or goTubs so I can pack just enough shampoo and conditioner to fit in my carry-on. I admit I hate checking a bag! I also refill where possible instead of having to buy endless travel sizes. However, I did find both hairspray and mousse in small sizes that I keep as part of home supply. I also go for MAC, Bobbie Brown, or any company that allows me to mix and match blush and eye shadow shades so I can limit my cosmetics to essentials.

A Woman's Perspective

Noise Cancelling Headphones

Want or Need?

In my case, noise cancelling headphones are an absolute need. A **Popular Mechanics** 2002 advertisement said it all, "Think of it as a mute button for the world around you."[9] Everyone has his or her favorite brand and style, and mine is the Bose QuietComfort headphones.

Unfortunately, noise cancelling headphones aren't cheap, and in my case, I'm buying a new pair every four years or so because they eventually wear out.

The reason I love my headphones so much is they truly block out the world around me. Since I work constantly when flying, I'm always listening to music to both energize me and create a sense of white noise around me as babies scream, dogs bark, and people talk nonstop.

---

[9] **Popular Mechanics**, September, 2002, Bose Advertisement, page 39.

Noise cancelling headphones are also very practical. When compared to listening to music on standard headphones, you'll find you can hear sound with clarity and at a lower volume. I also find myself more relaxed after a flight.

There are many brands and styles on the market at multiple price points. If you enjoy your music, watching a movie, or just the solitude that flying brings, invest in a good pair of headphones and you too will find these to be a must have for the seasoned road warrior.

I now carry in-the-ear noise cancelling headphones; light and easy for my bag, and I sometimes wear them at night when I have noisy neighbors. These are easy to slip in my bag. I also carry a spare pair, the kind that American Airlines pass out, for emergencies or when I lose the little rubber earpiece. I also have a white noise app, **Brainwaves**, that drowns out noise from the street. Asking for a room on a high floor helps too.

A Woman's Perspective

Workout Clothes

Working out while traveling always sounds like a great idea until you arrive to your work destination and the distractions of business meetings, the energy of a new city, and late business dinners are all in your way.

And then there's the luggage real estate your workout gear consumes. Taking a pair of running shoes alone could easily consume 25% of your packing space. For this reason, many people swear by their swim workout that only requires a bathing suit and goggles.

Either way, staying in shape is key to regularly crossing multiple time zones and waking up at 6:30 a.m. Eastern Time when your body says it's 3:30 a.m. Pacific Time, or the reverse when you're dining at 9:00 p.m. in Los Angeles only to hear your body scream, "It's now midnight and I need to go to bed!"

Travel Tip: Some hotels offer workout clothes including shoes at check-in. More hotels are catering to business travelers who like to work out. At some higher end hotels like Fairmont and select Sheraton properties, your workout gear is provided free of charge upon arrival, and some properties will deliver weights or yoga mats directly to your room.

They take some getting used to, but Vibrams are a light and 'skinny' workout shoe that work great. I also pack a flat Dyna-band (a latex exercise band) and download some awesome workouts on my laptop or tablet that don't require any equipment.

A Woman's Perspective

Travel Accessories and the Cable Challenge

Have you ever forgotten your power cables when packing? Your Bluetooth headset? Your phone?

Over time you will neglect to pack something important, and, like many of us, at some point you will lose one of everything. In my case, my Achilles heel is the cable. I either lost a cable or just didn't pack the right cable in the first place. Just like keeping a second set of sundry items, the answer here is to maintain a second set of cables used exclusively for travel.

Think about it. How many different technology products are you dragging on a business trip that require a separate cable? Here is my short list of required cables:

✓ Apple lightning cable for iPhone and iPad
✓ Apple 30-pin cable for iPod
✓ USB cable
✓ Micro-USB cable
✓ Apple MacBook power charger
✓ Male-to-Male 2.5mm pin
   (connects my iPod or my iPhone to my rental car radio)
✓ Power plugs
✓ Car power plug adapter

As I mentioned, I used to lose a lot of stuff until I decided full redundancy was the answer.

I now have dedicated cables for home use and dedicated cables for travel use. With this strategy, I'm no longer searching my house to find cables for a trip, and then unpack them when I return home. Cables are cheap and can be easily ordered online. This way my home cables stay home, and I always have the right ones on the road.

Of course, maintaining a "rat's nest" of cables and plugs in a bag is never easy. Yet, the rat's nest can be managed in a few ways. One is by organizing your cables using a system to keep your cables bound. A product called *GearTie* made by **Nite Ize** provides an easy and color-coded solution to cable management. The second way is to consolidate your cables into the right travel pouch. My accessory pouch is a 12" long shallow bag. The shallow bag makes it easy to fish out the right cable without taking all the cables out of the bag.

Now all I have to remember is to pack my travel pouch.

Travel Story: Too Many Bags, Courtesy of Scott Jones, Texas

I was launching the European operation for my employer, a technology startup, and had to meet my contact in London's Euston Station before traveling to a critical industry trade show.

He was late for our rendezvous, and I was nervous. Because I had a demo kit plus luggage, I had lots of bags to manage, and in my nervous state, I started to walk to the train without him. Along the way, I lost track of one of the bags. When I retraced my steps, I found the lost bag surrounded by British Transport Police Officers who were just about to clear the station and shut down all public transit around Euston.

My business contact arrived in time to watch me be chewed out by the police and almost arrested. Looking back, instead of trying to haul all of the bags alone, all I had to do was sit down, breathe in the air, have an orange (not coffee as caffeine makes you more tense), and wait for my contact to show up to help me carry the luggage.

Chapter 4: Cash and Credit Cards

It's very straightforward: when traveling, bring both cash and credit cards.

This is a simple concept, but accompanied by many complex caveats.

For starters, if your company is big enough, review the policy on company related charges. Even though the company credit card may be in your name, many companies have policies on what is and is not acceptable to place on your corporate credit card. Many companies also have policies on required charges to place on your credit card.

Nevertheless, despite a corporate credit card being a business asset, remember you are personally responsible for the expenses placed on this card. If your credit card bill is not paid, your personal credit could become damaged.

The majority of your business expenses will be your airline ticket, your rental car, and your hotel. The best policy is to always place these charges on your company credit card. This makes it easy to account for your business expenses, and provides a single monthly statement for your boss, auditor or accountant that only contains business expenses rather than a statement chock-full of both personal and business charges.

In addition to the credit cards always carry cash. Many times you'll be at a restaurant or hire a car where only cash is accepted.

If your company travel policy supports it, I suggest taking a small cash advance against your corporate credit card to pay for incidentals that you know will be reimbursed. For example, hired cars, tips, and meals often are cash only transactions. Mileage reimbursement if you drive your car to the airport is also a cash transaction as far as your expense report is concerned. In this scenario, your company floats you a business cash advance from the corporate credit card. Once you file your expense report, the advanced money goes back to paying off the credit card, and if applicable, many companies reimburse you for the associated cash advance ATM fee.

This strategy minimizes the personal cash required for a business trip. During a typical three-day trip, I can survive with

$150 of petty cash even if I'm traveling to a large and expensive city.

On the chance I need more money, I use my personal ATM card to tide me over until I am home, or I use my corporate card to take another cash advance. However, be careful about taking out too much cash from your corporate credit card, and execute this option strategically because too many cash advances could trigger a corporate audit.

Keep in mind **you will not make money or profit from a business trip** (some people do try to make money; read Michael Goldman's travel story in Chapter 14). Over time, there will be non-reimbursable expenses you incur, and there will be times your meal and post-meeting drinking budget exceeds your per diem field allotment. If you can break-even after a year of traveling, consider yourself lucky.

Many times in my career, and that of my colleagues, I have owed American Express thousands of dollars because over time my trip expenses exceeded my company reimbursements.

Here's why.

Over the course of a year, I took so many trips and filed so many expense reports, I felt like I needed a Masters in Accounting to keep track of all the debits and credits cycling through my corporate credit card. Also, once I found time to thoroughly review my credit card statements, I would find transactions either I didn't make or credits not received. The typical culprits? Charges for hotels or airlines that I thought I canceled or didn't receive credit for, as well as transactions I never properly expensed and received reimbursement.

The less you travel the easier it is to reconcile your corporate charged travel expenses, but the more you travel the more diligent you need to be monitoring your charges.

> **Travel Tip: Use your corporate credit card for all business travel transactions.** Forget the personal credit card reward points; over time, it's just not worth mixing your personal finances with your business finances.

Remember, even though you may not be doing a good job reviewing your monthly statement, if you work for a large company, you can bet some auditor is reviewing your corporate charge account for unusual charges. Charges made at strip clubs, bars, and head shops most likely will raise a red flag. If discovered doing something inappropriate, you could be placed in the position of losing your credit card, or worse, fired for incorrectly using your corporate issued charge card and violating company policies. And, don't use your corporate credit card to help make ends meet between pay dates. These exposures create an opportunity to "bet your job" since using your business card for personal charges violates most company expense policies.

If you are caught expensing something questionable never lie about it. If you lie, you'll *absolutely* be fired. Telling the truth at least keeps your honor, and gives you a better shot at keeping your job.

Early in my travel career, I hung my purse over a chair in a restaurant. Dumb! When I went to pay the bill, my wallet was gone. I spent the rest of the day cancelling all of my credit cards.

Now, I carry no more than the cards I need. Before a trip, I take every card out of my wallet and I photocopy them front and back. I keep the credit card company phone numbers handy too. To be extra safe, I leave copies of my itinerary, my first page of my passport, and my driver's license at home, and with a friend or significant other.

A Woman's Perspective

Travel Story: The Roadblock, Courtesy of Susan Schreitmueller, Texas

I was traveling in a third world country with big political issues, and I had to go for a visa. It was easy to obtain the visa at the embassy, but the route to the embassy was difficult. My young driver from the hotel was lost, and we ended up in a dicey side of town. Like a bad movie, sure enough we found ourselves held up by uniformed "officers."

As we approached the roadblock, I slipped most of my currency into my shoe and left about $100 in my wallet. The "officer" claimed that my driver's papers were out of date. As the poor kid was trying to explain, I thought he was going to be smacked by an AK47.

I took a deep breath, put on my best Southern belle lash-flash, and asked if I could help. When they said we were in violation, I naively asked if I could take care of the problem. Amazingly, the $100 in my wallet was just enough and off we went. To this day, I ALWAYS carry cash in separate places!

Chapter 5: Transportation to the Airport

How did something so simple become so complicated?

In the age of my parents, traveling to the airport was easy: someone drove you. Someone also picked you up.

Today, being driven to the airport by a friend or family member is a rare event. Life is too busy, it's inconvenient for the person you ask, and, in most major cities, the trip is easily an hour round trip adventure. Besides, the company typically pays for your transportation to the airport (or train station) and home again as a covered business expense. You are encouraged to validate this by reading your company's travel policies.

So here's your decision: drive versus bus versus hired driver?

While living in Boulder, Colorado, I knew if I drove, the trip to Denver International Airport was thirty-five miles each way. I could park onsite for $24/day, or offsite with a valet service for $14/day; the tolls were $8.25 each way, and it took me on average forty-five minutes from the time I left my house until I walked into the terminal door.

Meanwhile, a one-way taxi or a black car would cost me $90 including tip, while Uber would cost between $75 and $150 if I could find a car. This hired car option was typically thirty-five minutes door-to-door.

At the low end of the equation was the $8 one-way bus ride from my local Park-N-Ride. This took an hour and parking was usually free.

In my early business travel days, I would always take the bus. Then things happened outside of my control: wrecks on the highway, a bus broke down, long waits at the airport after I returned from a trip waiting for the next bus to leave, and no bus at all because I landed after the last bus of the evening had departed.

A taxi or a black car is a good, but expensive option until they don't show up. Uber and Lyft have even stood me up.

One time, after waiting fifteen minutes past my scheduled pickup time, I called my limo company. The dispatcher did find my reservation, but admitted they forgot to schedule a driver. Oops! I had to drive myself.

In major cities, subways are great, but similar to the bus, the ride time could be variable. The Blue Line between O'Hare and downtown Chicago is my favorite, especially during Chicago rush hour or heavy winter weather traffic. New Jersey Transit from Newark into New York City's Penn Station is also an excellent choice.

Do the math, but recognize your "go to" option may not work 100% of the time, and you should always be prepared to execute your backup plan.

Always think about the time you are planning to depart as well as the time when you are returning to your home airport. It is safer by far, to use pre-arranged transport if traveling very late or very early. When you park at the airport be "situationally aware," and park under streetlights. Also, consider hail (OK, I live in Texas) if you are using offsite parking. There was a time I came back to a severely dinged-up car.

Valet parking and pickup is nice if you have multiple terminals at your home airport. And most importantly, if you don't feel comfortable with a driver, call a friend and stay on the phone until you reach your destination.

A Woman's Perspective

Chapter 6: Airport Security

During a trip to Queenstown, New Zealand, I visited the Otago Region wine country. All the wine merchants told me I could buy wine and carry it on a domestic flight. I didn't believe them, but decided to take the risk. I bought a few bottles to test the theory.

A few days later, I boarded my Air New Zealand domestic flight from Queenstown to Nelson, and no one questioned me about my liquids. In fact, there was no security screening at all; I just walked on the plane.

Meanwhile, in the U.S., and most countries in the world, prepare for long security screening lines to be searched and to have your privacy and personal rights violated - all in the name of "security." After decades of travel, I easily accept this inspection as a way of life. To be blunt, I'm happy to be flying on a secure airplane.

With that being said, in the U.S. there are three ways to improve your security experience: 1) join TSA Global Entry or the TSA Precheck program, 2) apply for a CLEAR membership or 3) become an elite flyer.

I have both airport shoes and airport jewelry, and I hate to hold up the security line. I also pack for ease of access in case the TSA Precheck line is closed or I am randomly tagged for search. Also, PLEASE leave the heavy scents at home and don't bathe in the stuff. Your fellow passengers will thank you.

Always pack your batteries in your carry-on. You might have to gate check and don't want to have to dig for them at the last minute. Anything that looks dangerous should be carried in a see-thru bag and placed on top of your stuff. My favorite hairclip was flagged twice because it looked like a dagger in the x-ray machine so now the clip stays home.

A Woman's Perspective

TSA Global Entry and TSA Precheck

TSA Precheck is awesome! If you travel regularly, or even once a year, Precheck is a no brainer; moreover, if you think you will travel internationally, you want the upgraded government clearance called Global Entry which includes TSA Precheck.[10]

Think of Global Entry as TSA Precheck with an international option. Global Entry provides quick re-entry into the U.S. after your trip abroad. With Global Entry, there's no need to complete the customs and immigration form because

---

[10] For frequent travel exclusively between the U.S. and Canada, apply for NEXUS from the U.S. Customs and Border Patrol. If you have Global Entry, you do not need NEXUS.

you will do that electronically upon arrival at a Global Entry kiosk. No form means no waiting in a long immigration line.

Here's how the program works.

Complete the online application on Homeland Security's Global Online Enrollment System (GOES).[11] Once your application is accepted, schedule an appointment with a U.S. Border Agent for a live interview and fingerprinting. Unfortunately, scheduling the appointment is not quick and typically takes place at an airport. To give you an idea, my appointment was three months from my application date; however, I have been told if you go to an interview station, and the U.S. Border Patrol has time, they will squeeze you in.

At the successful completion of the interview, your fingerprints are digitized, and your Global Entry and TSA Precheck membership is completed. Your Global Entry membership includes a Known Traveler Number (KTN), and you can immediately use your credentials. Even though an identification card is mailed within a few weeks, the card is for reference only.

Be aware, just because you have TSA Precheck when flying United doesn't mean TSA Precheck is magically applied when flying another airline.

For TSA Precheck to be truly effective, you must provide each domestic airline you fly with your KTN. The easy way to do this is to include your KTN as part of your frequent flyer profile. The other option is to provide your KTN to an airline reservation agent when booking your ticket, or if available, when you make your online reservation.

When I fly for business, I use a corporate travel agent who has my KTN stored in my profile. During the early days of TSA Precheck, I found out my travel agent wasn't properly passing my KTN to my airline du jour, and my airline du jour didn't have my frequent flier profile either. This explained why I was not seeing TSA Precheck when I flew for business travel.

Personally calling the airline once your ticket is booked, or updating your frequent flier profile with your KTN are the only ways to ensure TSA Precheck. Also, the airline must be notified at least a few days before your flight. Don't wait to the last

---

[11] www.cbp.gov/travel/trusted-traveler-programs/global-entry

minute to provide an airline your KTN. Receiving TSA Precheck right before departure is nearly impossible since the TSA and flight reservation systems don't talk to each other in real-time.

TSA will tell you that even with a KTN, you aren't always guaranteed Precheck; however, from my personal experience, once my airline profiles were properly set up with my KTN, I've never been denied TSA Precheck on a U.S. domestic flight.

The cost for both Global Entry with TSA Precheck is $100 and the membership lasts five years.[12] The cost for TSA Precheck alone is $85.

Furthermore, if you are an elite flyer, such as a United 1K, or if you have an American Express Platinum Card, these organizations will reimburse you so effectively Global Entry with TSA Precheck is free. Each airline frequent flier membership program is a little different so don't be bashful about asking questions. Also, some companies are now offering Global Entry reimbursement as a company benefit.

If you just want TSA Precheck, many airports have small TSA offices where you can apply in person or you can apply online.[13]

Travel Tip: Get a Known Traveler Number. Your TSA Precheck or Global Entry number, or KTN, must be provided to your airline prior to your trip for TSA Precheck to work. Your KTN is the 9-digit number found in the upper left corner of your Global Entry card.

---

[12] Global Entry lasts for five years and you can reapply within six months of expiration. The expiration date can be viewed on your GOES membership homepage.

[13] www.tsa.gov/tsa-precheck

CLEAR

Before TSA Precheck, there was CLEAR.

In the TSA pre-Precheck era, when you entered airport security, CLEAR lines were short; moreover, after CLEAR authenticated you, you were lead to the x-ray machines in front of non-CLEAR passengers. And, sometimes you had an exclusive CLEAR-only metal detection machine.

CLEAR leverages security biometrics via an optical retina scan and fingerprinting combined with a background check. The disadvantage of CLEAR was the program was only available at a few select airports.

CLEAR went into bankruptcy in 2009, but reorganized and came back to life after being purchased in 2010.

Today, even though CLEAR is fully available at seventeen major and regional airports, the advantages to CLEAR are limited. At best, CLEAR could save a few minutes when compared to the occasional elongated wait when in a long TSA Precheck security line; however, as TSA Precheck lines do indeed grow longer, CLEAR's advantages will be greater for regular passengers at CLEAR airports. Again, CLEAR isn't everywhere or for everyone.

CLEAR costs $179 per year.

Elite Flyer

One of the perks associated with being an elite flyer is a preferential security line. Now, you don't see this at all airports, and this doesn't grant you the same reduced scrutiny offered by both TSA Precheck and CLEAR, but hey, you can take advantage of a reduced line and it's free with your elite airline status.

Travel Story: Protect your Eyeglasses, Courtesy of Pat Corcoran, New York

Sometime after 9/11, I was going through airport security and the TSA agent told me to take off my glasses (the first and the only time I've been asked). I was surprised, but I followed their orders and put my glasses in a small tray. I went through the body scanner with no problems and then waited for my stuff.

My laptop came out, then my luggage, but no glasses. I said something to the TSA agent, but I was ignored. Eventually, I attracted someone's attention; however, we could not find my glasses.

After five minutes of searching, I looked underneath the belt and found my glasses on the floor. Somehow my glasses were knocked out of the tray, and were destroyed by the rollers in the conveyer belt.

I am basically blind without my glasses, and I was traveling to a foreign country for four days. I would be in numerous meetings, and my entire trip would happen without my glasses.

Unable to have new glasses made, I purchased two sets of cheap reading glasses at an airport store so I could at least read. Not perfect, but this worked until I returned home.

Chapter 7: Pre-Flight and The Airport Lounge

After you pass through security, now's a good time to take a quick inventory of your possessions and make sure you have all your flying essentials.

Since you're not allowed to bring liquids through the security checkpoint, at a minimum your first stop should be for water. Becoming thirsty or dehydrated during a flight could be very uncomfortable so having your own personal water bottle is a lifesaver.

Even when sitting in first class, it's important to have your own water so you're not held hostage by turbulence or long delays on the taxiway. At your home airport, you can shop around for the best deal, but when on the road, be efficient and buy the first option available. Water will be equally expensive everywhere, so why waste your time trying to save a quarter? If you're eco-focused, travel with a high quality, BPA-free, water bottle with a solid lid, or leverage a single plastic bottle for the entire trip.[14]

The truly frugal eco-business traveler dumps the water out of the bottle before entering security and refills it at a drinking fountain.

Having some travel food is also equally important because you never know when your short one-hour hop becomes a five-hour ordeal due to weather, air traffic or maintenance delays. Either buy something before you board, or if you're thrifty and can plan in advance, stock up at the house on some serious travel food and grab what you need before you fly.

Pack nuts, fruit, healthy bars, fresh vegetables and even a few cookies or chocolates to help get you to your next meal. I've also found the food that I don't eat during my travels makes a nice afterhours buffet in my hotel room.

My personal favorite travel foods include: Triscuits, Apples, Pepperidge Farm Goldfish crackers, almonds and walnuts which I buy in bulk. Also, I often make a sandwich using frozen bread

---

[14] Check out the HYDAWAY collapsible travel water bottle as another eco-friendly, easy to pack alternative

so I don't have to spend crazy money buying something at the airport or eating airplane food.[15]

Which brings me to the airport lounge.

I am a big proponent of flying a single airline, and the consistent availability of airline lounges is a key benefit of flying a single airline (with a few exceptions like Southwest, JetBlue, or Frontier).

Airport lounges are member only clubs run by most airlines to accommodate their frequent fliers. I regularly use the United Club lounge over fifty times a year. Sometimes I'm in the lounge for ten minutes – long enough to download my email and hit the restroom – while other times, I'm in the lounge all day when flights are delayed or canceled.

These lounges offer free wireless, awesome and clean restrooms, free food, free newspapers and, in most cases, free alcohol.

> **Travel Tip: Bring Your Own Tea Bags**. Too often the flight attendant is passing me a cup of hot water and a low cost, crummy tea bag. If you're a fan of tea, keep a few bags in your carry-on.

Equally important, airport lounges significantly enhance my productivity while traveling. The lounge provides a personal workspace for conference calls and to both download and work my email. A lounge also provides a safe space to visit the restroom where, in most cases, I don't have to bring my bags into a stall. The airline lounge caters to the demographic of the complex traveler, and this means the clubs are both clean and quiet. Lounges also offer customer service representatives to help with air travel challenges in a calm setting.

And don't ignore the networking opportunities at an airport lounge. Lounges are amazing places to meet new people. I

---

[15] Using frozen bread keeps the sandwich cold for a few hours, and the bread is soft and defrosted after takeoff when I'm ready to eat.

continue to be amazed at the quality of people I meet, what they tell me, and even the amount of personal information they are willing to disclose to a total stranger. I've met friends I haven't seen in ages, entertainers, politicians, friends of friends, and even occasionally scored a sales lead. Nevertheless, remember you are representing your company, and you must always be on your best and most professional behavior. Even though the probability is low, you just might meet these people again.

Unfortunately, joining these lounges is not cheap. Without elite status, airline lounges are typically $500 per year; however, if you have elite status the price is prorated based on your level.

I feel like every time I travel, I overhear a person trying to talk their way into a lounge. Because of the high cost, and the exclusivity airlines like to maintain around their clubs, the days of talking your way into a lounge are over. Either you're a member, or you're not, and you need to buy a day pass. For reference, a day pass for American Airlines' Admiral Club or United Airlines' United Club costs $50 while the Delta Sky Club's day pass is $59. Always read the fine print about joining a club because each airline has a number of caveats and limitations.

No question, airline lounges are one spot on the travel roadmap where you have to pay to play.

Now, be aware some credit card companies, as a benefit, include an airline lounge membership, or access to an alternative airport lounge as part of their credit card annual fee. In the case of the American Express Platinum Card, you receive complimentary entry to American Express's Centurion Lounge, Airspace Lounges, Delta Sky Club, or Priority Pass lounges.[16]

Lounges like Centurion Lounge, and those offered through Priority Pass provide admittance regardless of which airline you're flying. Unfortunately, lounge availability and standards are not consistent, and your experience will vary between airports especially at smaller and remote international airports.

For example, when flying United in Denver there's no Centurion or Priority Pass lounge so I need to have a United Club membership or buy a day pass. On the other hand, when I'm flying United through San Francisco, I have multiple options

---

[16] Priority Pass is an airline lounge independent of airline.

including the Centurion Club and the United Club, and if I'm using the Priority Pass, I can walk over to the Air France-KLM Lounge in the international terminal.

As always, check out your airport lounge options before you fly.

Recently, a friend of mine traveled to Port-Au-Prince, Haiti on a first class, international ticket. Ticket Price: $2,500. Traditionally, if you are traveling international on a first class or a business class ticket, access to your airline's airport lounge or their partner's lounge in included in the ticket purchase. In this example, the representative denied access stating the Caribbean Islands didn't count as international access for a ticket originating in the U.S. However, when escalated to the airline's client service Twitter account, the airline representative said admittance was allowed. Long-story short, my friend ultimately gained access, but it was a battle due to the airline employees being confused on their admittance policy.

From a pure marketing perspective, if someone pays $2,500 for a first class ticket, it seems like a dumb idea to reject a traveler from an airline club.

> **Travel Tip: Purchase water bottles that have screw-on lids**. This may seem trivial, but bottled water with sports bottle style lids, or tiny screw-on caps often open up and leak. When using your BYO water bottle, after filling it up and tightening the lid, turn the bottle upside down and make sure there's no leak.

Travel Story: Playing the Standby Game, Courtesy of Michael Errity, Georgia

> *Since business travel around the holidays presents an opportunity, I wanted to see how*

many times I could be bumped from a flight, and how much compensation I could receive from my preferred airline.

During the 2015 Christmas season, I was traveling home from New York LaGuardia and the terminal was buzzing with people. Waiting for the gate agent to announce a "need for volunteers," I hovered by the gate desk; when the announcement came, I quickly approached the desk and offered my ticket. Boom: a $600 travel voucher. I then waited three hours for the next flight and hit repeat. Boom: a $500 travel voucher. I waited three hours for the next flight and repeated my approach. Boom: a $300 voucher! For flight number four 4, the airline team was on to my game. While waiting, a gate agent walks over to me and says, "Mike, it's time for you to go home and see your family."

I made $1,400 in fare credits just by spending a day reading, eating, and drinking in Terminal D at LGA.

Travel Story: Scotch Time, Courtesy of Michele Puldy Burger, Florida

While working in the Florida Legislature, my days were spent attending committee hearings and compromising with staff members and elected officials to pass proposed legislation.

For two years, as a legislative aide for a Florida senator, I worked on a complicated *draft with over 800 amendments. There was one senator who was a crucial vote, and his support was vital to this piece of legislation passing the Senate. Unfortunately, he didn't like my boss, and he refused our repeated meeting requests.*

At the end of one crazy week, the legislators and the staff members departed the Capitol to spend their weekend with family. I arrived late to the airport and missed my flight. Fortunately, I was able to secure a seat on a later flight, but I now had two hours to kill.

I decided to spend the time in the airline lounge where I ordered a scotch. The man next to me was surprised to hear a young woman ordering a single malt whiskey, and he was curious about my interest in scotch. Lucky for me that man was THE senator who refused to meet my boss. Outside our normal work venue, we spent the next two hours discussing his concerns with the proposed legislation.

Two weeks later, that bill passed both houses.

Chapter 8: The Airplane

For many people, the most critical, and the most thrilling part of the business trip is the airplane, or the actual flight transporting them from point A to point B.

The airplane ride determines if you make your business meeting, and if you are home in time for the Little League game or the Friday evening birthday party.

Here's another example where the importance of airline loyalty comes into play. Whether you are a United 1K, a Delta Platinum Medallion, an American Airlines Platinum Executive, or some other rare element, if you want to truly ease your travel pain, pick the best airline that works for you, and become an elite flyer with that airline as fast as you can.

Here's why being an elite flyer matters:

✓ Preferred check-in line

✓ Preferred call-in number (less time on hold waiting for an   agent)

✓ Free changes on flights made within 24-hours of flight time (based on availability)

✓ No charge to check multiple bags

✓ Priority rebooking when your flight is canceled or you miss your connection

✓ No charge and no blackout period when using award miles to book flights

✓ Priority bag sorting and availability upon arrival (your bag is out first)

✓ Preferred boarding (this means there is always space for your luggage)

✓ Discounted price to join the airline lounge

✓ Seating with extra legroom at no additional cost

✓ Free upgrades to business or first class

✓ Airline employees are generally nicer to you

Priority Check-in and Boarding

Selectively and randomly, the perks associated with being a high level frequent flyer will become important in their own way at the right time. However, I think the key benefits are priority check-in and boarding, being able to fly first class with some amount of regularity, and, most importantly, priority handling for flight changes.

Check-in and boarding is stressful, or it *can* be stressful if you're not thinking through your strategy. If I'm checking my bag, it should be checked about one hour before departure and labeled with a priority tag. The priority tag is key because it tells the ramp team my bag is the last on the airplane when loading bags, and one of the first bags at baggage claim when they unload.

On the other hand, if I'm not checking a bag, I want to be on the plane early enough so there's space in the overhead bin preferably near my seat. Nothing sucks worse than swimming upstream after the plane lands as you navigate from row eight to row twenty-eight to retrieve your bag. This means I board early when the first group is called to board the flight.

Flight Changes

Have you ever experienced a flight delay, a canceled flight, or missed a connection? If not, get ready and stay relaxed when your moment arrives because these things are like the weather; they happen and they are completely out of your control.

Your best defense in these situations is a good offense. Think smart, think quickly, and recognize only you can guide yourself through this problem.

When delays occur, most people go to the gate agent or to the customer service agent and ask them for help. While this works, typically there's a mile long line of people. This is especially common when an entire flight has been canceled or there's a massive weather delay. If you have status, you are provided a special customer service number which should be pre-programmed into your mobile's speed dial.

At the first sense of a problem, call this customer service line, and politely ask for help. The point here is that it's faster to call for help rather than waiting in line for the next gate agent. And, if you have elite status, your private number more times than not lands you an agent without a wait. However, there are exceptions.

For this reason, even if there are only a few people in line, don't be afraid to work the phone while you stand in the short line. Sometimes the person behind the counter knows things the customer service rep on the phone can't see. Occasionally, I've had both the phone rep and the gate agent working my problem at the same time, and in a crux the more people teaming to resolve your situation the better. Sometimes you act as the go-between while other times just hand the gate agent your phone while your personal rescue team finds an answer.

There will be situations when you're on a plane, waiting to take off, and, the engines wind down when they should be revving up. Like clockwork, next, you hear the captain declare there's a maintenance problem and the aircraft needs to return to the gate. While the other travelers are complaining, this is your cue to immediately work the phone, call your airline, and find another flight.

These days all flights are booked to capacity so there are limited extra seats; therefore, when problems occur keep your expectations low. The airline has a contract with you to deliver you where you need to go so it's just a question on how and when they can make that happen.

Having your special number is equally important when you want to make a travel change on your own. When I originally book a flight, I choose the flight that either has the best departure time based on my known schedule, or I choose a flight with the least expensive fare. Fast-forward to my day-of-travel, I might decide to leave earlier or later because my schedule has changed. With premium status, in most cases, flight changes are easy and often free.

Look at flights online to see when and where seats are available, find your best flight time and then call your airline. You may be surprised at your options. Your original flight that had a connection could become a nonstop, or your 6:00 a.m.

flight now leaves at 2:00 p.m. Seat options may not be great, but at least you are on the flight you want.

Remember, the airlines have their own problems every travel day: maintenance issues, schedule delays related to weather, customers with missed connections, and overbooked flights. When you change your flight time, you could be helping both the airline and another passenger who doesn't have as many options. Realize there's a symbiotic relationship happening with day of travel changes. You are helping yourself when you change your travel time, and because many times it benefits the airlines, they are happy to help you too.

> I check the weather before I fly (and always keep an eye on it if dicey), and have my backup plan for hotels if I think I will be stuck. I am also on the phone with the American Airlines Executive Platinum desk to protect a seat on a different flight if flights are delayed. Weather, invariably, also causes gate or even terminal changes.
>
> A Woman's Perspective

Flying First Class

Everyone's favorite perk is flying first class!

There's status, prestige, your friends and family are impressed, and it's almost like eating a free meal at a decent restaurant when upgraded because you feel special. Unfortunately, every year there are more frequent fliers competing for the same first class seat, and airlines try to sell those seats up to the last minute before the gate agent closes the door. The competition is fierce, and every year, I find it harder and more complicated to score a free first class upgrade.

Decades ago, I heard stories of how people talked their way to a first class upgrade. Today, that's impossible. Your only true upgrade options without buying a ticket are: 1) use frequent flyer points or 2) fly with elite status on a high revenue ticket and upgrade via the airline's priority system.

As a 1K, I'm flying first class 33% of the time. This means one out of every three flights I'm upgraded, but this also means two out of three times, I'm flying in my pre-assigned coach seat. It's depressing to see my name number one or two on the upgrade wait list when I check-in twenty-four hours before my flight, only to see my name drop to twelve by flight time because higher revenue tickets and ultra-elite fliers were prioritized ahead of me by the computer. What I really hate is at check-in someone spends the additional money for a last minute first class seat, and I lose my perceived seat up front.

Anyway, the formulas for who is upgraded is both complicated and controlled by a computer and a computer programmer. The harsh reality of upgrades is if you don't have elite status, or you aren't willing to actually pay for an upgrade, there is no easy path to first class.

Depending on the airline, when you arrive at the gate you'll see the flight information monitor display an upgrade list. Many airline mobile apps also include the upgrade list with the flight status information. Sometimes I am listed as number one on the upgrade list, but the first class cabin is declared checked-in full; however, I don't give up hope because even when on the plane the gate agent may find me and move me to the front row.

On multiple occasions, a gate agent has found me in my coach seat and presented me with a first class ticket.

And, in one instance, while the gate agent was upgrading people around me, I was bold enough to stop the agent and ask why I wasn't being upgraded. I showed her my phone app and pointed out I was number one on the upgrade list. Checking her print out, she apologized for missing my name, and I was immediately moved to seat 1A.

Flying first class is so choice!

Achieving Elite Status

Now, there are a few ways to expedite becoming an elite flyer. The first is to request probationary elite status, and the second is to apply for the airline's credit card.

In some cases, you can call your preferred airline's frequent flyer customer service center and request "probationary elite status." If approved, the airline will give you sixty or ninety days to fly a certain number of flight segments, a specific number of miles, or spend a minimum amount of money. The airline may also request a copy of the membership card of the airline where you currently have elite flight status.

Many years ago when I lived in Tucson, Arizona, I switched from Delta to American Airlines, and American granted my elite probationary request. However, this doesn't always work. When I tried the same tactic in Singapore, Singapore Airlines told me the only way to gain status was to actually fly the miles.

In the case of Singapore Airlines, I decided to continue with my United 1K status, and always flew Singapore Airlines under my 1K membership. Since they both were of the Star Alliance airline consortium, I received every perk on Singapore Airlines that I received on United except one. I received: club access, preferential check-in, preferred boarding, and all of my air miles went towards my United flying status. Unfortunately, I never received a complimentary upgrade on Singapore Airlines.

If you are living overseas and plan to fly that country's host airline, do your research and make your own decision. Sometimes staying with the airlines alliance is the way to go, but other times, it's best to start from scratch and switch airlines. There are many blogs and chat rooms oriented towards answering this question.

Clearly, this is another first-world problem for today's expat.

> **Travel Tip: How to pack a suit.** If your trip is brief, wear your suit pants and jacket on the flight. At a minimum, wear your jacket on your flight. Once on the

plane, turn your jacket inside out, fold it in half and place it on top of your luggage. This keeps the outside of your suit from being stained, reduces wrinkles and avoids the possibility of a stranger crushing your jacket with their stuff. Also, use those dry cleaning plastic bags to pack your clothes in your luggage. For whatever reason, the plastic reduces wrinkles. Women carrying a garment bag should ask the flight attendant if there's a place to hang the bag in the first class coat closet.

> If I check a bag or I am flying international, I travel in clothes that, in a pinch, could be worn to the client site. I don't want to shop for something at the last minute.
>
> A Woman's Perspective

Travel Story: Celebrity Sighting, Courtesy of Michael Errity, Georgia

After a sleepless weekend celebrating my youngest sister's wedding, I was delighted to receive the upgrade to first class. Sitting in seat 1B, the flight attendant taps me on the shoulder and says, "Sir, your seatmate is going to be a celebrity – please don't call attention to him. "

Exhausted, and uninterested, I fell back asleep. Minutes later, I am tapped on the shoulder again, but this time I need to let the person slip into 1A. I stand up and look into the chest of Charles Barkley. I smile and say, "Hello, Charles. "

He had just hosted Saturday Night Live. Charles was carrying a large pizza, which was ironic because at the time he was a spokesperson for a weight loss company.

I dozed off and on through the flight. Charles was just the nicest, most genuine guy anyone could imagine. No pretense, no hesitation, and generous to everyone coming by. As we deplaned, he wished my sister and brother-in-law a lifetime of happiness.

Chapter 9: Arrival

You've Arrived!

Literally.

I've always felt arrival at a new airport and a new city to be one of life's most disorienting experiences. Once you leave the safety of a secured airport terminal perimeter, anything is possible. Someone can mug you in the restroom, or you make the mistake of taking a ride from one of those guys softly asking you, "Need a ride into the city?" Next thing you know, you start imagining you are in the midst of your own horror movie where the driver locks the doors, and he's driving you in a direction that completely conflicts with your map app.

Relax, the reality is make good choices and nothing bad will happen; however, it doesn't hurt to plan your arrival in advance, and like your mother told you, "Be weary of strangers."

Transportation

Different cities around the globe offer different transportation options. I always prioritize safe and quick options over the least expensive. Remember, your safety and comfort is always paramount when you're traveling for business. Your focus needs to be on your business meeting, and the last thing you need is to be distracted by screw-ups before arriving to your hotel.

In most cases in the U.S., a rental car is the best option. The car can either be retrieved at the terminal, like in Jacksonville, or you might need to take a bus or train to the rental car pickup zone like in Seattle or Phoenix. The big downside to a rental car is you need to be able to navigate on your own, and parking is expensive. In cities like Chicago, Los Angeles, New York or San Francisco, you can expect parking bills as high as $50 per day. Even at some hotels, such as near the airport in Atlanta, a hotel may charge you $15 to $20 a day just to park in their empty lot. There also could be valet charges in the city, parking charges at the client, surprise toll roads, and don't overlook the need to refill the rental car with gas before you return or there's another surcharge to your rental.

After the rental car option, the next best choices are subways, trains, taxis and rideshares like Uber, Lyft, and SuperShuttle.[17]

To be honest, wherever possible, I take subways, trains or leverage the taxi/rideshare option, and while rental cars provide lots of convenience, it's my last option. Knowing the city makes the decision easier. When traveling to larger cities like New York, Chicago, San Francisco, Washington, D.C., or others with very good mass transit, the subway/train option makes sense.

If I truly want to know a big city, and where possible, I exclusively use the subway. Taking subways allows you the opportunity to become acutely familiar with the city, feel like a local, and receive the added bonus of exercise. You also gain some street cred during your business meeting when you let your hosts know you arrived like a local.

Also, don't be afraid to mix it up. Perhaps the best option is a taxi to and from the airport. But, once in the city, the subway makes the most sense for intra-city transport with an occasional cab when you don't have time to mess with mass transit.

For example, when I fly to New York, I prefer to fly into Newark and take New Jersey Transit into Penn Station at 33rd street between 7th and 8th avenue. I then either walk to my midtown hotel, jump into the subway, or take a cab. Taking the train into the city is just as fast, or faster than an airport cab, but significantly less expensive.

Remember to buy a return trip ticket to save time when it's time to leave the city and return to Newark Airport.

For those occasions when you are staying at an airport hotel, forget the rental car and the taxi, and look for the airport hotel shuttle bus. Most offer complimentary transportation to their property.

Before closing this chapter, here's a good moment to mention safety and rideshares. While it may be cheaper to take the least expensive option, like UberX, think about taking a higher end, safer option such as UberBlack. UberBlack is a

---

[17] When taking a taxi at the airport, always find the taxi queue and do not accept a ride from a solicitor. Accepting a ride from a non-sanctioned driver could be significantly more expensive not to mention a safety concern.

professional chauffeur service; moreover, all UberBlack drivers carry commercial car insurance, an airport permit, and a Transportation Charter Permit (TCP). Needless to say, UberBlack is very different from UberX cars that are driven by just about anyone with a driver's license and a decent car. Once again, when on business travel remember "safety first."

Travel Tip: Don't leave your laptop bag in the rental car when you valet park. It's easy to leave your laptop bag in your rental car, but valets have access to your car, and they may not be careful locking your parked car. Also, if your rental car is stolen or lost, you may never see your laptop again. For another perspective, security experts will tell you to never leave your laptop in your parked car at any time.

Always have the address of your hotel (printed out in local language if necessary) with you. There is often more than one Hilton/Marriot/Doubletree in the same city.

Know the cell phone driving laws of the state you are visiting. A headset might be required.

Check for a "tolltag" device. This will save you headaches on bridges and toll roads. If the transponder isn't in your car, ask your rental company to supply it.

Consider taking a CD slot phone holder. You may be trying to navigate in New York traffic holding your phone – not a good idea!

Pre-program your hotel and client destination into Waze or Google Maps.

Take the time to check for any pre-existing damage to your rental car and adjust the mirrors before you leave the rental car lot.

A Woman's Perspective

Travel Story: Lost and Found, Courtesy of Steve Gilbert, Florida

During a trip to San Diego, as we were handing our rental car over to the hotel parking valet, my colleague and I collected all of our valuables. When my colleague opened the center console, she found a black bag literally full of money.

We were shocked. The bag contained a brick of cash wrapped in white paper. At the hotel, I dialed 911 and told them my story. The police said they were too busy and would call me back in five hours. Feeling uncomfortable hanging on to that amount of money, I drove to the police station myself.

At the police station, the cop at the desk opened the brick of cash and counted six-hundred and fifty $20 bills, or $13,000.

About this time, I checked my voicemail, and there were seven messages from the rental car agency manager stating that someone was frantically looking for a lost item in my rental car. I happily made arrangements to return the money to the rental car agency, and my problem was now their problem.

Chapter 10: Hotels

When booking a hotel, find one that balances proximity to your business meeting, comfort, loyalty points, and naturally, price.

At large companies, procurement has negotiated amazing room rates with a handful of hotels, and these companies will require you to stay in their company-approved hotel. This is a good news, bad news situation. The good news is you typically receive a comfortable hotel room at a sometimes ridiculously low price; moreover, some amenities like breakfast and free internet are often included in the deal.

The downside is you need to stay in these hotels, and there is no other option. Also, the location may not be optimal to your business meeting requiring you to wake up earlier than normal so you have enough time to get there ontime. But perhaps the worst part of these deals is the hotel has the option to place you in whatever room they want. Despite my premier status at nearly all of the hotels I stay while on business, I continue to be amazed when I'm placed in the room for people with disabilities that is closest to the elevator.

I really hate this because the room closest to the elevator is typically the noisiest. I have been woken up many times by a loud group headed to their room after partying all evening. Also, I feel like I'm parked in a space reserved for a handicapped driver. What if someone shows up who really needs this room?

Which brings me to hotel loyalty.

The best thing you can do is apply for a loyalty card to every hotel you stay in even if you think you will only stay in that hotel chain once a year. In many cases the points you earn with that hotel chain never expire; moreover, just by having a loyalty card, many hotel chains give you perks like free internet, free breakfast, and free minibar.

Here's a real life example on why this is important.

A friend of the family just graduated from college and took a job with a consulting firm. An early assignment for her was six months working with a client in Beverly Hills staying at the Beverly Hills Marriott. It's not the Beverly Wilshire, but the Marriott is a nice hotel in a nice location. For six months, she arrived every Sunday and left every Thursday. Each time she checked in counted towards her next level in Marriott's loyalty program, and every night also counted. By her third visit, she was a Silver Elite. By her fifteenth visit, less than four months, she reached Marriott's Platinum Elite level. Once there, she received amazing rooms, wine and flowers upon arrival, and they would always let her check-in early and leave late. Essentially, she became Marriott royalty. Between her status and all the earned points, she earned a free week at a Ritz Carlton anywhere in the world!

In short, she became an ultra-elite client for Marriott. Once you reach that level, hotel chains take extremely great care of you, and you can expect a holiday card every December from your new best friends.

Despite all these nice perks, staying in hotels isn't all glamour. After all, you're in a hotel. The rooms are small, you don't have your stuff, and there are strangers all around. I have countless stories of hearing people screaming in the room next to me. While this may sound titillating, and it does make a great after the fact story, typically, I'm not in the mood to be listening to someone else's party when all I can think about is working my one-hundred awaiting emails.

The nice hotel room can also feel like a prison cell. A nice prison cell, but a cell just the same since you feel stuck in a small space and there's no food. Be wary of arriving late at night; the hour when it's too late to find a restaurant.

On the plus side, most business hotels offer room service until 10:00 p.m., and the good ones offer a limited food option well after midnight. Of course, ordering room service is ultra-expensive, and the bill is often double what you see on the menu.

Why? Expect a delivery charge and a 20% service charge added on top of that. And, always read your check before you award your server a tip. The service charge represents the server's tip so be careful about tipping twice.

Also, remember to keep your dining expectations low when ordering. The crab salad may sound great, but unless you're in Boston, stick to something basic and healthy, and you know you'll enjoy even under the worst conditions. For me, the Cobb Salad or the Club Sandwich is always a safe option. A basic hamburger without the bun also comes with a high probability of success. Think of hotel food as simple food exclusively designed to bridge you to your next major meal.

> **Travel Tip: Always ask for a room upgrade** Asking for a room upgrade at a hotel is completely different than asking for a cabin upgrade on an airplane. Room upgrades are given out all the time. Be bold and ask if there's an upgrade available every time you check into a hotel because the worst that can happen is they say, "No." As a wise traveler once told me, "If you don't ask, you don't get."

The Workout

Do you workout? If yes, don't let your business travel stop you. At a minimum, it's easy to workout in your room, or if the weather is nice and you're in a good location, it's fun to explore the area near your hotel.

Also, many hotels have workout rooms, and for the hotels that don't, on occasion, you'll find they have a relationship with a nearby facility or your home gym has a reciprocal arrangement with their locations in other cities.

On the flip side, bringing your workout stuff is complicated. My running shoes alone could take up one-third of my carry-on luggage, and often I am so busy I never use them. Nevertheless, it's important to find time for fitness when you're on business travel.

During short trips, it's easy to skip a workout; however, when you're on the road for a week, or staying over a weekend, in order to keep fit for life and for traveling, it's important to find a way to include your workout (and your workout clothes) as part of your routine.

If bringing all your gear isn't practical, check if your hotel supplies workout gear upon arrival; or, maybe the hotel has a pool, or a relationship with a gym that has a pool, and you can bring your bathing suit. Pound for pound, a great swim will kick your butt. And don't worry if someone sees you in a swimsuit because everyone's a stranger. For times when you can't wait for your suit to dry, carry a dry bag and wash your suit at home. This too may seem slightly inconvenient, but in the end you'll enjoy some great exercise and feel better about that heavy business meal you were forced to experience.

Travel Tip: Go for an early morning walk or run A great way to explore the city is go outside right after sunrise before you dress for your day. There are few people and few cars, and you can observe a city when life is peaceful and quiet. Use the time to look for interesting restaurants or bars that you could visit for dinner or drinks that evening. Also, you may find unique shopping opportunities otherwise missed once the day becomes congested. To help, there are several apps to plot routes for a walk or run. Here are some: **MapMyRun**, **FootPath, Localeikki,** and **CoolRunning** for local running groups.

During the warmer mornings in Chicago, I often run on the path next to Lake Michigan and enjoy a healthy dose of the morning city vibe.

As every knows, don't run alone in an unfamiliar place when it is dark. Be particularly careful of dark alleys. If you have doubts, there are many great workouts for your tablet or laptop. Pack your Vibrams and go for it! We have to be more cautious than the guys, and like a broken record, please be situationally aware. What is the neighborhood like? What is your gut telling you? Does the hotel feel safe? Always use the deadbolt on your door. There are too many hotel staff members with master keys or duplicate keys. I always check my room thoroughly and even pull the shower curtain back just to be 100% certain I'm alone.

Once, I left my reserved, company-approved hotel and paid for one on my own because my company's preferred hotel gave me the heebie-jeebies. Turned out they had several muggings there hence the fence and Bruno – the security guard.

A Woman's Perspective

Travel Story: Bad Hotel Room, Courtesy of Chris Pantano, New York

During a business trip to Harrisburg, PA, I selected a corporate hotel chain that was usually a safe bet. When I arrived, the hotel had a large bus outside the front entrance. At check-in, the clerk tells me the room I requested was given away, and the only room left was a smoking room.

Upon entering the room, there was a large ozone machine and a spray bottle on the table. Within five minutes, I saw jumping bugs. The room was invested with fleas.

Grabbing my stuff, I returned to the front desk and requested another room. The clerk said they were totally sold out. I asked for the manager, and since it was late, I was not going to search the town for another room. I told the hotel manager he needed to provide me a bug-free, sanitized room or I was sleeping in the lobby.

He said he could not help me. I waited for fifteen minutes before I decided to take off my shoes in front of the desk. I turned my briefcase into a pillow and lay down on the floor. The manager said I couldn't sleep there; however, after a few minutes, he miraculously found me a nice bug-free, non-smoking room.

Chapter 11: Dining and Meal Policies

There's no question, business travel is a lot of work. For every night you're eating at a four or five star restaurant, there are four nights you could be eating at Chipotle, Subway, IHOP or Waffle House. Regardless, if you take the time to find a fun place to eat, you'll find your travel experience that much more rewarding. I know people who arrive in a city and never leave their hotel except for their business meetings, and that seems like such a waste of a potentially great experience.

Before the days of restaurant location apps like **OpenTable**, **Yelp, TripAdvisor**, and **LocalEats**, my primary search method was running or walking the city. Trust your intuition, and chances are high you'll find a place that's unique, local and one you thoroughly enjoy.

Of course, you're not on vacation. This is business, and more times than not, you have a lot of work. Yet, as easy and tempting as it is, don't be weak and order room service. Taking an hour for dinner outside of your hotel won't impact your productivity, and besides, you have your phone or tablet to keep you connected.

While eating out all the time sounds great, be prepared to eat on a budget. Many companies provide a food per diem for their traveling employees. In short, the company determines how much money you have per day to eat. Unfortunately, there's no standard and every company handles per diem differently. Some companies don't even offer a per diem, and they reimburse you for actual expenses up to a limit.

Companies that have no limits and just reimburse you for actual expenses are rare. Typically, startups have no meal policy; consequently, at some point they are financially burned. The ones with no limits quickly create caps as more employees travel. One person told me her company reimbursed her $75 per meal for working in Los Angeles. I said, "Oh, $75 per day is not bad." She quickly corrected me and said, "No, I'm reimbursed up to $75 per meal per day." Wow!

At the other end of the spectrum, there are companies that have incredibly low per diems, and only pay for breakfast and dinner. Even if you normally eat lunch at home, or brownbag at the office, when you travel you could be on your own for lunch. Other examples include companies who request you to deduct breakfast or dinner if someone else is paying on your behalf, or if you eat for free at those "breakfast included" hotels. While I guess these policy caveats make sense from an accounting point of view, these exclusions seem designed by someone who isn't on the road seventy-five days a year and has to eat by these policies.

In any case, it's very important that you know the rules of your company and follow them closely. If the company demands receipts for your meals, or highly recommends you place your meals on the corporate credit card, just do it. The last thing you want is for a corporate auditor to be asking you about an unusual meal charge from eight months ago.

Also, in the case where someone at the table picks up the meal for the team, don't commit fraud by trying to collect for a meal expense that you didn't incur. These are bright red flags when auditors pick up on the fact multiple employees are in the same city, and visiting the same client on the same day.

In today's world where everything's traceable, the per diems are minimal, and the auditors appear to be everywhere, it's not worth betting your career on the $25 you make by collecting a per diem on a meal someone else paid for, or perhaps food you never ate.

The person who tries to make money while on business travel is fooling themselves; thinking one can make money traveling for business is an equation that just won't close. Traveling on business is at best a break-even experience. People spend money on stuff they can't expense, and the time and the aggravation associated with travel often makes the trip not even worth going. In short, it takes a special person to want to constantly travel for business, and making money off the travel expense budget is just not enough to move the financial needle.

If you are in a job that requires you to travel, and you don't like the rules, then you might be in the wrong job.

Keep in mind, people are fired for violating corporate meal expense policies. Don't be a travel policy casualty.

Travel Tip: Bring cash for the team drinks and the team dinner. At some point, you'll be eating dinner with a large group and while you may order frugally, others may not. There's always someone who decides to order the lobster along with four pints of beer. Typically, the total bill from these large dinner checks is divided equally amongst everyone present. Do you see the problem? If you aren't interested in subsidizing someone else's meal bring cash.

Travel Tip: The Starbucks Effect. There are times when I just don't know what to eat or where to go. Even with ten travel apps at my disposal, I am so brain dead, or indifferent, even the apps don't help. As a way to jumpstart my thinking, I look for a Starbucks using their mobile app or my maps app. I don't necessarily want to go to Starbucks, but I know their coffee shops are typically placed in high traffic locations where there are lots of fun places for people to shop, eat and drink. This isn't just a U.S. statement, but something I've experienced worldwide. So, next time you're in a funk, look for a Starbucks, and you'll be surprised at what you discover.

Travel Story: An Italian Dinner in Italy, Courtesy of Steve Gilbert, Florida

While traveling with a group in Milan, Italy, we asked our local host for a restaurant recommendation. Although she wasn't available to join us for dinner, she happily provided us with a suggestion.

When we arrived, we realized the staff spoke no English, and the menu was entirely in Italian. After several unsuccessful attempts to communicate with the waiter, he said, "un momento" and walked away. Within minutes, our waiter returned with his team carrying plates of food.

Throughout the night, they continued to bring out one sumptuous course after another. I'm not sure of the names of the dishes, but it was one of the best meals I ever had.

Chapter 12: Returning Home

Good news! Your business meeting was a roaring success. You feel awesome, and it is time to go home.

The night before I travel home, I pack the majority of my things so it's not a crazy rush the morning of my hotel departure. This is especially important when catching a 6:00 a.m. flight. I know I won't be thinking clearly when I wake up at 4:00 a.m. to shower, dress, and pack. Too many times, I've left things in hotels like coats, toilet kits, chargers, Bluetooth headsets, and Kindles.

I discovered the hard way that anytime I can pack the night before, the higher probability I will pack all of my things. There are even times I make a list of all the items that need to be in my travel bag before walking out of the room. And, it's a good idea to start the ritual of walking the room, opening all the drawers, looking for stray adapters plugged-in, and scanning the closet just one more time before leaving the room. My Mom use to do this when we would go on family road trips, and I thought this step was silly. However, it only takes one time to leave your noise cancelling headphones to figure out this "last minute check" is a good practice.

Also, it's good idea to look at the final hotel bill before you actually leave the hotel. Many hotels now send electronic copies instead of sliding the bill under your door, and too many times I have found movies, mini-bar, restaurant, and other incidental, but incorrect expenses. It's easier to debate these in person with the front desk clerk, or on the phone from the comfort of your hotel room, than to deal with bogus charges a few weeks later while filing your expense report. You are on the hook for these charges until you contest them, so don't be afraid to argue your bill.

Travel Tip: Don't leave the key in the room at checkout. There have been times, as the room door slams shut, I realized I forgot something in the room, and I left my key in the room for the maid. Having the room key in your possession, as you leave your room for the last time, makes it easy to pop back into the room. You can quickly reclaim your stuff or receive peace of mind that everything is properly packed.

When returning a rental car, I allow myself at least fifteen minutes extra time to dump the car and catch the shuttle bus or the airport train to the terminal. If I need to refill the gas, which costs a fraction versus having the rental car agency refill the tank for me, then I do that the night before. Even if I have to drive twenty miles to the airport, in most rental cars that's not even a gallon of gas.

In the days before 9/11, I worked for someone who would drive her rental car to the terminal and just leave the car at the terminal entrance. She, or her assistant, would then call the rental car company from the gate area and tell them where they could collect their car. It's hard to imagine this happening today.

Depending when I arrive at the airport, I also try to build some time to stop at the airline lounge. Even if I only have 10 minutes, I will stop at the lounge. As mentioned earlier, lounges provide free food and drinks, and the restrooms are safe and extremely clean. Despite all of these nice amenities, the real reason for a stop at the lounge is the free and fast wireless internet.

Not everyone has a high speed LTE or 4G plan for their laptop or their tablet. And while I have an internet hotspot on my phone, there have been too many times it has failed me because someone decided to send a twenty-megabyte PowerPoint as the airplane door was closing.

Chapter 13: International Travel

International travel is one of the most gratifying, educational, and confidence boosting life events you will ever experience. While I'm very comfortable traveling internationally, I exercise caution on every trip to maximize my health and safety because while it's great to have an international adventure, it's equally gratifying to return home.

Before you leave any country, you need a passport. Passports must be current, have empty pages for stamps or visas, and must have an expiration date greater than six months from the time of your departure.

While rare, I continue to hear stories and see people stopped at the airline counter or at immigration because their passports don't meet these requirements. Also, while you can expect the airlines staff to check your passport multiple times at check-in and while boarding the plane, they are not the experts. Don't expect that just because the airline staff says your passport is in good working order that the immigration official will have the same opinion.

Also, if you have an existing passport, check the expiration date. Even if you don't have a trip planned, make sure that your passport is renewed long before it expires. For whatever reason, it's easier to renew a current passport than one that has expired.

The biggest reason you want a current passport is you never know when your company will need you to make a last minute trip to London, Paris or Shanghai.

Too many times, I've looked to my employees to travel overseas only for them to tell me a) sorry, I don't have a passport, b) my passport has expired or c) if you pay for my passport then I will apply for one.

That last comment really upsets me because it just screams complacency. Show some leadership! Show some commitment to your job! If you don't have a passport apply for one, and if your passport is about to expire, renew it.

A first time U.S. passport costs $110, and if you need to expedite your passport it could cost another $80. Add the price of photos and miscellaneous expenses, and the cost for a rushed passport is over $200. U.S. citizens can submit their passport application at most U.S. Post Offices. The standard turnaround to process a passport is four-to-six weeks, while expedited service takes roughly three weeks; however, if you live in a city where you can go directly to a passport agency or to a consulate, it's possible to receive a passport within eight days. As expected, there are agencies who will run your passport through this expedite process, but prepare to pay hundreds of dollars above the U.S. State Department fee for this service.

For U.S. citizens, consult the U.S. State Department for more information.[18]

Also, while most countries have gone to "e-visas," eliminating the need for you to send out your passport, it's still important to have plenty of blank passport pages. Missing a blank page, or having a torn passport page, is enough for an immigration official to deny you entry into their country. For that reason, when you apply for your passport, there's an option to order extra pages. There's no reason not to order them, and the extra pages are free if you order them at application time. At a minimum, you'll have a fat passport that looks different than everyone else's and adds to your international travel coolness.

Now, if you're fortunate enough to have a job that requires a significant amount of international travel, and you're a U.S. or United Kingdom citizen, then it's worth applying for a second passport. When I lived in Singapore, I traveled almost weekly, and there were many times having two passports made the difference between traveling to see a client or staying home and losing business.

Separately, if you have dual citizenship, and thus have passports from two different countries, you might have the two passport issue already solved. On the other hand, if your second passport is from a country that's not widely accepted by most countries, then your second non-U.S. passport may not be so helpful.

The U.S. and the United Kingdom are two of the few (and perhaps only) countries that allow its citizens the privilege of possessing two national passports. Requirements to obtain a second passport are specific, and it's possible to get one from a local consulate while you're out of the U.S. For example, I

---

[18] travel.state.gov/content/passports/en/passports.html

picked up my second passport at the U.S. Embassy in Singapore during my expat days. The process was easy, and there was even a photo booth at the Embassy.

There is virtually no downside to having a second passport, and the U.S. State Department recently increased their lifespan from two years to four years. Even though this isn't as good as the ten-year life provided by regular passports, the four-year lifespan increases flexibility in supporting your international travel needs. Again, consult the U.S. State Department website for more information.

In addition, always travel with extra passport photos. When I take passport photos, I typically purchase a dozen at a time. I'm always traveling with extra photos in my bag because I never know when a passport photo comes in handy. Passport photos are small, weigh nothing, and are great to have in a situation where you lose your passport and need a quick replacement. Passport photos are also required for most country entry visas, and there's been more than one time when I've had to apply for a visa while on the road. Keeping digital passport photos on your phone or laptop could also prove helpful.

Finally, I know this is repetitive, but I can't stress enough how important your passport is to your travel life. I hear too many stories about passports being picked out of purses on metros, stolen at restaurants, and even forgotten in the hotel safe after checking out of a hotel.

When on the go, maintain a constant vigil on the whereabouts of your passport, and keep it on you when and where it makes sense. One common option upon arrival is to place your passport in the hotel room safe, but recognize this isn't always a good idea. I'm especially sensitive to the political climate of the country, and the safety feeling of the city before I make a decision on whether or not to leave my passport in the safe. Don't fall into a false sense of security just because you're staying in a five star hotel; a passport could be stolen from your room regardless of the hotel brand.[19]

Also, think about the business day ahead of you. There are times I'm visiting a secure client location, and in order for me to

---

[19] Weisel, Al. Travel+Leisure, *How Secure is Your Hotel Safe?*
www.travelandleisure.com/articles/how-secure-is-that-hotel-safe

enter a building, I need to show my actual passport; neither a driver's license nor a company identification card is considered acceptable proof of my identity.

Travel Tip: Take a picture of your passport. Take a picture of your passport with your phone, and email it to a close friend or loved one. In the terrible circumstance of a lost passport, a replacement passport is quickly expedited when you can show proof of your former passport. This includes your passport number, date of issue, date of expiration, and your photograph. Also, if you have special visas, take pictures of those too. You never know when you need proof, and having a picture of your passport declaration page on your phone, or a printed hardcopy, can make a world of difference.

The Mobile Phone

When I first started traveling internationally, mobile phones were science fiction. The only way to communicate for business was email, and even that was spotty. Today, of course, mobile phones are ubiquitous, and in most cases, your domestic phone will work without any problems on an international trip.

The big challenge, however, is to economically use your phone while traveling. For travelers with European or Asian based phones, many plans provide low cost international options for voice, SMS, and internet. More importantly, these phones are "unlocked" - meaning you can swap your SIM card out for a local SIM card. Yet, for U.S. consumers, the majority of their phones are "locked." Therefore, when traveling with a U.S. phone, you are locked out of using a foreign SIM card. Also, you are forced to either pay crazy rates to your U.S. provider or rent a local temporary phone that works in the country you're visiting.

With the introduction of the CTIA's Consumer Code for Wireless Service, at some point, at your request, wireless companies in the U.S. are required to unlock your phone; however, the conditions are not easy.

Complicated? Yes, but hang in there and let's cover the options.

Unlocked vs Locked Phones

As I mentioned, the majority of U.S. phones, or "handsets," are sold "locked." This means if you have an AT&T phone, you will have an issue using your phone if you switch to Verizon before your contract expires. The Verizon network, and the Verizon SIM card won't work in your AT&T phone. An unlocked phone allows you to easily switch providers simply by swapping out the SIM card on your current phone.

In many countries around the world, the country network provider (sometimes there are multiple) allows you to buy a SIM card so your phone will work on their network. If you have an unlocked phone, and you replace your U.S. SIM card with a local in-country SIM card, you instantly have a phone that works in that country on their local mobile network with a local in-country number.

Let's use Australia as an example. If you have an unlocked phone upon arrival in Melbourne, before leaving the terminal, drop by the Telstra shop, and in ten minutes your phone can be up and running on the Telstra network. Telstra allows you to buy a plan that conforms to how you think you'll use your phone in Australia.

How many gigabytes of internet traffic do you need? How many SMS's will you send? How much actual talk time will you require? Since most people have no idea how to answer these questions, the decision is best made on price. For example, ask the Telstra sales rep, "How many gigs for AU $50?"

The nice thing about Telstra is they have a website and a mobile app so it's easy to add gigabytes and minutes to your plan as needed while you're traveling within Australia.

Another benefit of a local sim card is the local number making it easy to communicate with local business colleagues and clients while in the country, and there's no issue calling local restaurants, museums or cabs; moreover, your new Australian friends can easily call you back. Plus, always having active internet means your Google Maps and Uber easily and inexpensively work. And, since you are using your phone, all your apps, contacts, and email system are in the palm of your hand.

The downside is your home country phone number goes dead, and all calls to your U.S. phone number go right to voicemail until you put your U.S. SIM card back in your phone.

I found it's better to have a local SIM card with low-cost working internet, SMS, and a local voice number than to have a working U.S. phone number. When you're on the other side of the planet, all your co-workers are asleep and won't call you during your day. Of course, if my friends and co-workers from my home base want to call me, I can provide them my new international phone number.

At night, swap out the SIM cards and check voice messages, see who called, and SMS people during their day so they can call you from the U.S. on your U.S. number. Be aware that while it will costs nothing for people to call you, unless you have an international plan, your fees will be wildly high as you pay international long distance fees plus roaming charges to your U.S. provider.

Unfortunately, not every country allows you to swap out your SIM card. Each country has its own laws on mobile phone use. Swapping SIMs is easy throughout the European Union, but especially tough in some countries in Asia and in the Middle East, so do your homework before you travel.

Regardless, you MUST have an unlocked mobile handset for the SIM card swap to work. If your handset is locked then you need to either work with your mobile provider to unlock your phone, or go to eBay, Amazon, or an applicable retailer, and buy an unlocked phone. Either way, if you plan to use your handset on another network, in another country, **you must have an unlocked phone.**

One other point: unlike the U.S., in many countries around the world, most people do not use voicemail. You'll find their voicemails are turned off, or they just don't bother to pick up messages. Consequently, if you call someone's mobile, and they don't pick up, don't be concerned. Either call again later or just send a SMS. Everyone uses SMS of one variety or another.[20]

> **Travel Tip: Don't expect Toll Free 800 or 888 numbers to work outside of the U.S.** U.S. toll free numbers do not work when dialed from outside of the U.S. or Canada. Consequently, find the non-toll free number for any business you think you'll need to call while out of the country. Most credit cards have their direct number (+1 + area code + seven-digit number) printed on the back of their credit cards, but not all. Sometimes I am able to make a U.S. toll free call using Skype or GoogleTalk, but not always. Be ready!

The Business Travel Visa

Before purchasing your airline ticket, find out what type of travel visa you need. Just so everyone is on the same page, a visa is a stamp that goes in your passport, or an electronic approval that allows a person to enter a foreign country under a specific

---

[20] If you're looking for a completely different approach, TravelCell offers mobile phone rentals that work in over 200 countries. Rent an iPhone or an Android, get a U.S. number, and have unlimited email and internet while you travel internationally.

passport. There are many types of visas, and the way you apply varies by country.

If you need a visa, complete the application, find your passport photos, and then mail your passport with the completed documents to the closest consulate or embassy. In a week or two, or three, your passport will be returned with a nice looking stamp on one of your blank visa pages.

A small number of countries, mostly in Asia, offer "visa on arrival." In this case, a visa can be secured when you arrive at your destination airport, but before you pass through immigration. Bring a pen to complete the application and some U.S. dollars in small denominations.

Another option is the electronic visa. The immigration form is completed online and you will receive a confirmation number with an email. Remember to print a copy and hand it to the immigration officer upon arrival.

Finally, there are the countries where you don't need a visa at all.

As you can guess, there are many websites with answers to which type of visa is required. The host country state department website is a good starting point. There are also external companies which provide this detail. They provide up-to-date information on the type of visa required based on your type of travel and nationality, passport services, and they will also expedite obtaining your specific visa and making sure your passport is returned before a trip.

Regardless of what type of visa is required or how you apply for it, I want to stress the importance of being knowledgeable and prepared on your visa needs well before you arrive at your destination. Nothing stinks more than traveling for 22 hours only to be told by the immigration officer, "Sorry, your papers are not in order, and I can't let you into the country."

Immunizations

When traveling domestically in the U.S., a current tetanus and the immunizations you received as a child are probably good enough; however, if you're traveling internationally, think long and hard about immunizations. Malaria, Hepatitis, Rabies,

Typhoid, Yellow Fever, Zika and other exotic diseases are no joke and should be taken seriously. Also, travelers who are trying to become pregnant, male and female, should maintain an even more heightened sense of awareness.

Before you travel, the **U.S. Centers for Disease Control and Prevention** is the go to place to figure out what type of immunizations are critical for your trip. In many cases, your employee insurance plan will cover the costs, and for common immunizations, your local doctor can inoculate. Yet, for more complicated immunizations you may be redirected to a company that specializes in immunizations like **Passport Health**.

Looking for an Anthrax vaccine? **Passport Health** is the company for you!

If you're like me, you have no idea what vaccinations you received or when, and this is where the "Yellow Card" comes into play.

Approved by the World Health Organization, the "Yellow Card," or "International Certificate of Vaccination or Prophylaxis" is a yellow document, about the size of a passport, which fits in your passport cover or easily in your pocket. The Yellow Card becomes your proof of vaccination when traveling between countries – especially those at risk for Yellow Fever. For example, in Africa, the Yellow Card is commonly requested at both port of entry and port of exit where infection and disease is a high probability.

Medical and Medications

No conversation on international travel would be complete without a discussion regarding medical treatment and medications.

When traveling domestically, besides traveling with your prescriptions, most people give zero thought to their health. The U.S. water and air supply is high quality, your body is used to your normal foods, and it's very rare someone will catch food poisoning while on a domestic business trip. Sure, people become sick when traveling, but the issues related to health are generally common, and in most U.S. cities, reputable hospitals and emergency rooms with a highly trained staff are available.

Moving the focus from domestic to international travel, the thought process changes significantly. For starters, before traveling to a foreign country, once again consult the **U.S. Centers for Disease Control and Prevention** for the latest information on the country you plan to visit. And, for added value, review the CDC's page on *packing smart* where the CDC outlines specific medicines to consider for your trip. Passport Health is also a good source for medicine options.

Some travelers take a small pharmacy of over-the-counter drugs with them when traveling internationally. A standard medicine arsenal includes: Benadryl, Imodium AD, Tylenol, and Sudafed. Taking the pharmacy concept one step further, several of my friends bring a minimal set of antibiotics too; however, there isn't one size fits all when it comes to antibiotics, so this is a hit or miss strategy. I highly recommend going to the CDC website and the Passport Health website for education, and then talk to your doctor to understand the best options.

In terms of medical options, meaning clinics and doctors, this is a trickier subject. Most business hotels have a doctor on call, or can refer you to a medical center frequented by westerners with western trained physicians. And yes, the CDC site, *Getting Health Care Abroad*, is a natural stop when looking for medical assistance. For business travelers who work for larger companies, in some cases, these companies have an international business travel program that will find you a doctor and a pharmacy; and moreover, in the worst of cases, provide a medical evacuation option. Not exactly the best time to be taking your first ride on a private jet, but it's a welcome option in a terrible situation.[21]

---

[21] A number of travel insurance companies and premium credit cards offer emergency evacuation insurance. American Express, Travelex, Allianz, AIG are a few options. If you hold a high-end credit card, such as an American Express Platinum Card, it's possible you already have emergency evacuation insurance, but always check before you travel.

Packing and Dressing for an International Flight

Once your flight departs, on most international flights you have between eight to sixteen hours of airplane time. Looking left and looking right, odds are high you do not know anyone on the plane so this is a good time where function beats fashion. In short, become comfortable quickly so you can relax, read, sleep, and eat as if you're in your pajamas and bunny slippers back home.

If you've checked your bag, carry some spare clothes in your personal carry-on. A sweatshirt, long flexible pants, and a warm pair of socks are perfect. If you're in business or first class, the airlines will provide socks, a toothbrush and toothpaste, and in some cases even pajamas. As soon as the seatbelt sign is off, change clothes before the bathrooms become busy.

I'm amazed how my flight experience improves when I'm in a pair of loose yoga pants or doctor's scrubs rather than wearing jeans or dress pants. Also, it's easy to feel cold on long flights so I always bring a sweatshirt or a loose fitting flannel shirt. A heavy scarf is also a good idea especially for women. This is not the wardrobe to wear when trying to impress your boss flying up front, but when you're by yourself or with friends, you will be the envy of those around you.

The reality is, after a twelve-hour plus flight, you're not going to feel great. Between the jet lag, the lack of sleep, and the overall disorientation associated with a long international flight, any advantage is important.

Travel Tip: Change back into travel clothes about two hours before landing. Lavatories are busy right before landing so it's important you change into your street clothes plenty of time before arrival. The airline's meal service begins about two hours before landing so coordinate your wardrobe change to avoid clogged aisles from flight attendants delivering meal service. This is less of an issue if you're flying business or first class.

Drinking and Eating Abroad

When traveling internationally, you need to recognize eating and drinking is not the same as dining in your home country. Specifically, the food and water supplies may not be as pristine as you are expecting, and, if you're not careful, you could become violently sick with food poisoning, diarrhea, or worse, you could pick up a bacteria or parasite that can only be cured by an antibiotic. In some cases, you could become so infected that your life could drastically change for the worse.

Did I scare you? I hope so, because eating and drinking overseas is serious business.

Now, the good news is you don't have to be that nervous everywhere you travel. In modern and developed countries like Canada, the United Kingdom, most European countries, Japan, Singapore, Israel, Australia and New Zealand, you are perfectly safe to drink the water and eat the food. While it's possible you don't like sea urchin sushi in Japan or vegemite in Australia, at least you know the food is safe to eat.

Which brings me to what it's like in developing countries. Some areas of Africa, Asia, India, and South America should be on your watch list. Do not eat food that isn't properly cooked, and be careful about drinking tap water. If you are not sure the water is safe, do not brush your teeth with water from your hotel sink; moreover, when showering, keep your mouth shut and be careful not to accidentally swallow water coming out of the showerhead.

In these countries, bottled water is the standard. Your host may occasionally offer filtered water, but depending upon the location, politely thank them and show them your safe bottle of water. Also, many hotels advertise filtered water; however, I like to be extra careful, and even though the hotel water may be perfectly safe I don't take any chances. These hotels will often have several free bottles of water in your room.

Taking this precaution one step further, watch for ice in your drinks. The ice may or may not be safe, and as it melts, your once safe glass of water could become contaminated.

Be careful, and when in doubt, at all times drink bottled water and no ice in your mixed drinks.

Next, let's address food. If you choose your hotel wisely, the food should be safe. Food at the larger chains such as Marriott, Hyatt, Fairmont, and Hilton can be generally counted on for safe, quality food, but there are exceptions. When staying in a local smaller hotel use your judgment. If the food is properly cooked your problems should be minimal to none. Raw fruits and vegetables that need to be washed should be avoided. Fruits that are peeled or have a shell like bananas, watermelon and oranges are ok.

To make this simple, as long as the food is properly cooked, and you feel confident the food hasn't been contaminated with the local water, odds are very high you will remain healthy. The real challenge with eating, however, is not in the hotels. The biggest risk comes from eating in local restaurants, or places your host takes you for lunch and dinner. In these cases, I'm always polite in choosing my food, but I keep my guard up.

For starters, I always order bottled water at the restaurant, and I want to see the bottle opened at my table. Beer, wine, and hot drinks are also safe. Looking at the menu, I focus on foods that are grilled, baked, or sautéed, and stay away from salads and undercooked meats and vegetables. Cakes and cookies for dessert are typically acceptable, but be careful of fruits. If you are faced with a buffet, use your judgment. Simply put, anything that looks sketchy, no matter how awesome your host tells you it tastes, should be avoided.

Throughout my decades of traveling, I have always followed these basic rules and I have never been sick – even during my dozen trips to India.[22]

---

[22] Checkout Foodsafety.gov for tips on food safety and how to eat safely when traveling abroad

The Currency Question

A common question when traveling internationally: "How much cash should I bring?" The answer is always "it depends." Now, despite that vague answer, my standard is $150 in U.S. dollars, two different credit card types (e.g., one Visa and one American Express), and at least one card that has international ATM access to withdraw local currency on demand.

Upon arriving in any country, besides making sure you have your luggage and know your method of transport to your hotel, number three on your list of arrival action items is to have some cash in local currency. Your country of arrival will determine if $150 is enough, or perhaps you need more. In short, a good rule of thumb is to bring enough cash to support your entire first day of arrival. This includes transportation, meals, and if applicable, tips. This will give you time to find a local ATM to increase your local cash reserves, and validate where your credit cards work.

In most international airports, you can exchange your U.S. dollars or your national currency after immigration, and then reclaim your national currency when you leave the country. Hotel reception is also an easy place to exchange money; however, keep in mind exchange rates at both the hotel and the airport are not as good as rates found at banks, ATMS, and kiosks located in town. Look for a good currency application for your smartphone to understand the latest exchange rates.

Ideally, everywhere you go use your credit card. This limits your cash exposure, meaning less money you have to carry around on your person, and you have a record of your expenses when it's time to file your expense report. If you are going to a big name, modern city, almost all taxis will accept credit cards. Trains and subways from the airport also accept credit cards; however, if you are in a less developed or a less technologically advanced country like India, have cash ready. Even in modern countries, there is always the problem where your ride doesn't accept credit cards and you can't Uber from the airport to your hotel.

Even when I take a taxi in modern places like Singapore or Paris, there are times my ride will only accept cash. So, just because you're in one of the most modern countries in the world, don't expect the technology to always work.

Finally, before you travel, contact your credit card issuer, let them know you are traveling to a foreign country, and request a fraud exception on your card for the country and the dates you plan to travel. Nothing is more embarrassing than paying for a business dinner in Beijing only to have your credit card rejected. Furthermore, while American Express advertises they allow their card can be used internationally without a pre-travel phone call, if you are visiting many countries in quick succession, it's a good idea to give them a heads up.

Also, check with your issuer for possible international transaction charges. Even though in most cases these charges are considered business expenses and you can place them on your company's expense report, the better solution is not to have these charges in the first place. American Express, Capital One Visa, and other Visa Signature cards do not charge transaction fees for international purchases, but as always, check and confirm before you travel.

Travel Tip: Understand currency exchange options and rates before you land. In most countries you can easily exchange money at the airport upon arrival, and convert the local currency back to your national currency upon departure before you enter immigration. However, I've found in some airports there are no exchange kiosks or banks in the airport main hall or the departure hall. In these countries, their currency is so poorly valued they maximize keeping your valuable U.S. dollars. For example, the Buenos Aires (EZE) airport has no place to exchange money upon departure, and if you're not careful, you could be stuck with a lot of Argentinian pesos.

When traveling internationally, I carry *two* ATM cards as sometimes one card doesn't work. I also call the issuing bank to have my cards authorized for the appropriate countries. Using an ATM will give you the best exchange rate. Remember, leftover cash can always be used against your hotel bill.

A Woman's Perspective

Immigration and Baggage Claim

Upon arrival, the first order of business is to clear immigration. This can be easy or difficult. If you have the correct visa and a current passport (expiring greater than six months from your date of travel) with blank visa pages, you should clear immigration quickly.

In some cases, the immigration officer will ask you a series of questions that you should answer succinctly and quickly. This is not the place to make friends unless the immigration officer likes to make small talk. You could be asked questions like:

✓ Is this your first trip to our country?
✓ Where are you staying?
✓ What's the purpose of your visit?
✓ Where were you before you came here?
✓ What's your job?

✓ Who do you work for?

✓ How long will you be in the country

Since your documentation is in order, there's no need to be nervous; most of the time, the immigration officer will barely say hello, and you'll be through the gate in thirty seconds.

With the potential for long waits, many countries have created electronic immigration check-in programs. As discussed in Chapter 6, the U.S. program is called **Global Entry.** With Global Entry, you receive a Known Traveler Number (KTN), and you can use special kiosks upon arrival which expedites your entry into the U.S. The TSA has created reciprocal programs with a number of countries including: Australia, Canada, Germany, New Zealand, the Republic of Korea and the United Kingdom. This means if you have Global Entry, you MIGHT be able to bypass the long lines and use a foreign country's electronic immigration process.

Here are some examples of Trusted Traveler programs outside of the U.S.:

Australia	Smartgate
United Kingdom	UK Registered Traveler Program
Germany	EasyPass-Registered Traveler Program
APEC Member Countries	Asia Pacific Economic Cooperation (APEC) Business Travel Card

If you are traveling to one of these countries, check with the *TSA Trusted Traveler Program* to validate you qualify.

After you make it through immigration, remember to collect your checked bag. Because there are so many black square bags, or gray big bags, or whatever your preference, it doesn't hurt to place a bright color piece of yarn, rope or even a special tag or monogram that easily allows you to identify your bag from far away.

When leaving the departure hall, in most airports, you may encounter exit choices of a green lane (no duty payment) or a red lane (duty payment required). The majority of the time, you will go through the green lane. This means you aren't importing goods, such as alcohol or cigarettes, into the country beyond the local limit. If you go through the red lane, you need to declare your excess, and the customs officer will calculate your tax on imported goods.

Here's another opportunity to have your travel unexpectedly disrupted.

Please understand the laws of the country you are entering so you know what you can and can't bring into the country. Equally important, understand what goods can leave the country. For example, in the U.S., it was illegal for many years to import Cuban cigars.

Most countries look for the "sin stuff" like alcohol, tobacco, and illegal (and legal) drugs. Just because the drug you are taking is legal in your home country doesn't mean it's legal in the country you're visiting. Read about the Toyota Executive arrested for importing Oxycodone into Japan.[23]

In some countries, even though you see a red lane and a green lane, there's really no choice, and the customs officer will inspect everyone and screen every bag. One time when entering Singapore, my bag was randomly x-rayed and they saw a large knife. The officer asked me if it was for cooking, which it was, and he let me through. I'm sure if I was importing a Japanese samurai sword, the conversation would have turned out differently. There are many stories where Singapore custom agents find excessive amounts of cigarettes or alcohol, and if you don't confess when caught expect a fine and your goods confiscated.

Most importantly, NEVER bring an illegal drug into a foreign country. An extreme example is in Singapore. The Singaporean government imposes the death penalty for importing illegal drugs into their country.

Be respectful of the local laws, and you'll always be in good shape.

---

[23] www.wsj.com/articles/toyota-executive-reportedly-arrested-for-drugs-in-japan-1434624904

Travel Tip: Run, don't walk to the immigration queue. At larger airports, many international flights all arrive around the same time, and that places a strain on the number of immigration officers working the entry gates. Imagine four Boeing 777s full of people all arriving in Seoul at the same time. This means roughly 1,500 people are entering the country simultaneously; furthermore, they all need to be processed by the same eight immigration officers. Don't be surprised if you have a 45-minute wait to pass through immigration - just like waiting to ride the Matterhorn at Disneyland!

Take a landing card from your flight attendant before you arrive. If you can't, just grab a blank when you approach immigration and proceed to the counter. Don't stop to fill it out – you will probably have time in line. And, don't take pictures in the immigration hall no matter how tempting that selfie might be upon landing. You can lose your phone, or worse, be detained. Also, be very careful about bringing food into your destination country. Fruits, cheeses and meats typically trigger violations. One of my friends spent eight hours in an Australian customs holding area because he was carrying a piece of cheese.

A Woman's Perspective

The Airport Car

The first time you arrive in a new country and at a new international airport, the experience can be quite overwhelming. Jet lagged, lots of people, new languages, new customs, and even the restrooms and food served in the restaurants are different. Between being jet lagged and your senses operating on a high state of alert, it's easy to be confused and disoriented. Arranged transport to the hotel can make all the difference with the initial success of your trip.

Consequently, one item I found that makes entry easy is the "airport car," and the simplest way to arrange an airport car is to contact your hotel.

While in many airport taxis are less expensive than a pre-arranged car, there's rarely a wait for the airport car. Either your driver or an agent of the driver has your name (or your hotel's name) on a sign outside the departure hall. Once you connect with your contact, you are quickly and safely taken to an awaiting car. In some cases, the car has a wireless hotspot which is a nice bonus.

The key words here are "quick" and "safe."

There are too many stories of taxi drivers ripping people off or taking passengers to the wrong destination; therefore, in my mind, and considering most companies pay for your airport to the hotel transportation anyway, there's no downside to using an airport car.

Don't assume your taxi driver will speak English. Take a printout of your hotel's name and address with you in the local language. This is especially important in character based language countries like Japan and China. Also, when you leave your hotel, take a hotel card with the address in the local language. Sometimes the taxi drivers have limited reading skills, but they will recognize pictures and key street names.

A Woman's Perspective

Dealing with Jet Lag

If you have issues when you fly from New York to Los Angeles, a mere three-hour time change, wait until you attempt a sixteen-hour nonstop flight from Newark to Hong Kong across twelve time zones.

When you fly from the U.S. to Asia, your flight lands in the afternoon or early evening local time so it's possible to sleep after arrival since it's their evening. The problem is your body wakes up around 1am local time, and while your mind wants rest, your body is ready to go to work. On the flip side, most flights from the U.S. to Europe land in the morning which means by 4:00 p.m. you're ready for bed while your European colleagues are thinking of the best pub to start the evening.

As you can tell, jet lag is a serious challenge, and despite what you may think or hear, every person responds differently to the jet lag experience. In short, everyone has their personal way to deal with jet lag.

Here are actions I take to combat jet lag:[24]

✓ I dress comfortably and change into sleepwear for the majority of the flight

✓ I drink a few glasses of wine, watch two movies, and sleep one-third to one-half of the flight

✓ I wear a watch, and immediately upon take off, set my watch to the new time zone so mentally I am already thinking in a time that references where I am going (for example, if I take off at 9:00 a.m. ET, New York for Singapore, I know to set my watch to 9:00 p.m. local Singapore time, and I need to sleep by 2:00 a.m. local time)

✓ On rare occasions, I take an Ambien or comparable sleeping pill, or maybe Dramamine (check with your doctor to see what makes sense for you especially if you plan to drink alcohol)

✓ I use an eye mask and some earplugs, or noise cancelling headphones to eliminate distractions

✓ If the flight isn't crowded, I look for a row where I can lie down

---

[24] These are the actions I take when traveling. Before consuming alcohol, taking medicine or doing anything physical, please consult your doctor. What works for me may not work for you.

✓ When arriving at the hotel, if it's not late, I go for a walk and acclimate myself to the new air and surroundings, or sit in the lobby bar and watch the crowd

✓ If I wake up in my hotel room at 1:00 a.m., I stay in bed, calm my thoughts, meditate, and do anything and everything to force my mind to go back to sleep

✓ I take a long, hot shower or bath before going to bed

In the end, the most important thing to do is condition your body to your new time zone as quickly as possible. This means forcing yourself to stay up late at night, and staying in bed as long as possible in the morning. Typically, within three to four days, your body will be running perfectly.

> **Travel Tip: Upon arrival, take a shower.** If I need to start my business day immediately upon arrival in a new country, I will take a shower and shave before meeting my airport transport. Fortunately, many international airports and airport clubs have shower facilities that you can rent for a short period of time. These are operated by either airport hotels or by the airport themselves and cost between $15 and $20. No reservations are required. Check the airport or your airline club website for details.

Travel Story: Jet Lag Reality, Courtesy of William Hahn, California

On a trip to Paris, after a greatly delayed flight from Los Angeles, I arrived at the five star Le Meurice Hotel on the Rue de Rivoli around 2:00 a.m. for a short stay before flying to Istanbul. I went and when I woke up there was a weak sunlight outside the room, and snow had collected on the windowsill. I called reception and asked, "What time is it?"

The receptionist replied, "5:30."

"5:30 in the morning?" I responded.

"Non, monsieur, it is 5:30 in the afternoon, Are you okay?"

Travel Story: A Long Day in Paris, Courtesy of Don Platt, Alabama

It was 1981, and I was traveling from St. Louis to Nairobi, Kenya.

The flight path was supposed to be St. Louis to New York City to London to Nairobi; however, because of the Air Traffic Control strike, the flight to New York City was canceled and Trans World Airlines (TWA) rerouted me STL-Boston-Paris-Nairobi with the Paris to Nairobi leg flown by Kenya Airways which was code sharing with Air France and TWA (a big red flag).

I arrived Paris early the next morning at Charles de Gaulle Airport. Since the Kenya Airways flight was from Orly Airport, I needed ground transportation via a bus to Orly.

Arrived at Orly around 8:00 a.m. and the Kenya Airways flight was at 10:00 p.m. At the airport restaurant, I was forced to check my briefcase, and the menu was entirely in French. Eventually, I managed to eat a cheeseburger (with no bun) and french fries.

Bought a Rubik's Cube to help kill the next twelve hours.

I kept checking the Kenya Airways desk for my flight status, and somewhere during the day, I discovered my TWA booked flight from Paris to Nairobi left the day before.

Kenya Airways sent me to the Air France desk, and Air France told me to straighten this out with TWA. Since TWA had no presence at Orly, I was forced to take a taxi back to Charles de Gaulle. Back at Charles de Gaulle, TWA booked me on a second flight, and I took a taxi back to Orly. Later that night, I flew Paris to Nairobi.

On the positive side, I solved the Rubik's Cube after several dedicated hours.

Chapter 14: The Expense Report

Welcome back to work!

Within a week of returning to your office, all of your travel expenses will have hit your company credit card, and it's time to file your expense report. As a reminder, while your company card is issued on behalf of the company, you are personally liable for the charges. If you take your time submitting your expense report, or if your company delays paying your credit card company directly, you are still personally responsible for these credit card charges and your personal credit might be impacted.

Most expense reports can be submitted in fifteen minutes or less, and it's in your best interest to submit them quickly. For starters, some companies have expense submission policies requiring you to turn in your report within a specific time window. Also, your travel expenses go against someone's travel budget for the month, the quarter, or the year, and no manager likes seeing surprise expenses months after they were incurred.

When completing reports, an easy temptation is to game the system. As expense reporting technology has improved, software can now easily tie together corporate charges with your expense report; consequently, "illegal" charges, like dinner at Spearmint Rhino, are quickly flagged as suspect and sent to company auditors for investigation. In short, if you try to post bogus charges thinking you can make a few extra dollars by submitting cash expenses for tips and parking, or for taxi expenses you never incurred, think again. Companies monitor their travel costs more closely than ever because these are expenses that are considered discretionary and can be controlled. The last thing you want is to lose your job for either expensing unsupported charges or making travel decisions that violate company policy. For example, flying to Orlando to spend the weekend at Walt Disney World when your business meeting takes place on Tuesday in Tampa is not a good choice without management approval.

It's imperative that you are well schooled on your company's travel policies. If there's a manual, then read it. If the company is small and there's no manual, ask questions and find out what's acceptable and what's not before you travel. Even for companies without travel policies, staying at the Ritz Carlton or the Four Seasons, when your CEO and CFO always select Hilton or Klimpton properties, might be a career-limiting move. Know your company policies for hotels, flights, transportation, and meal limits before you travel, and don't learn them while trying to complete your expense report. Worst case, you are fired, and best case, you may place yourself in the position of paying for your own expensive travel education.

Here are my seven rules for company travel:

1. Always accept the lowest fare airline on your company's travel website
2. Only stay in company approved hotels
3. Always accept the approved rental car class from the approved rental car agency
4. Never expense beyond the corporate defined per person business meal limit
5. Keep receipts for everything, and store them in a folder or an envelope from the hotel so they can be easily found after you complete your trip
6. Always use the company travel tool or agency to book your flights, hotels, and car rental
7. Always use your company issued credit card to pay for flights, hotels, and car rental

If you follow these seven basic rules, you'll successfully stay out of corporate travel jail. One more important rule: I file the expense report within ten business days from the conclusion of my trip to minimize angry emails from my corporate credit card company telling me my account is past due.

Remember to keep hard copies of your hotel bills from foreign countries that collect a value added tax (VAT). Your company will want the tax refund.

Long ago, I started my habit of taking a manila envelope on each trip to store my itinerary and receipts. On the outside of the envelope, I write the amount I paid for my air ticket and the expenses as I incur them (e.g., taxi to airport – 20 Euros). I note any ticket exchanges, and I slip my receipts inside the envelope. I also use my phone to take pictures of receipts when I'm not traveling internationally.

A Woman's Perspective

Travel Tip: Lost luggage? Work the airline and not your employer. I had an employee who went to China, and the airline lost his luggage. As a stopgap, he bought nice new clothes in China and placed these charges on his expense report. His charges were not reimbursable. Most companies will not reimburse lost personal items even while on business travel; however, most airlines will provide some financial reimbursement to help you cover a fraction of your personal loss.

Always keep your checked baggage claim barcode, and a picture of your luggage snapped on your phone could be helpful too.

I always take a picture of my bag along with the bag claim tag. Once, my luggage was lost between airlines in Africa, and this was the only tracking available. Remember to take any prescriptions in your carry-on (along with glasses and other non-replaceable items). And again, always have a copy of the Rx script in case you are questioned about prescription meds, and understand a country's list of forbidden prescription drugs.

A Woman's Perspective

Travel Story: Supplemental Income, Courtesy of Michael Goldman, Georgia

I worked a project as a young guy where I was paid per diem.

The understanding was whatever I didn't spend, I was allowed to keep. Since my salary wasn't that great, and I was paying Washington, D.C. rent, I learned to roll cheap. I learned to jam very economy.

If my hotel allowance was $55 a night, I routinely found hotels for $20 a night, and a week on the road could net me a couple of hundred bucks.

One trip I went too far.

On the outskirts of Baltimore, I found a hotel close to my project for $12 a night, $14 a night if I didn't return the key. This was the kind of place where characters from a Tom Waits song went to die.

I convinced myself I could do this, and I slept in a sleeping bag over the rust colored sheets. On the first night, eventually, I nodded off only to be woken at midnight by what sounded like a tornado of exploding glass. The entire room was shaking. Trying to figure out what was going on, I went to the back window, and I saw a passing train.

The hotel was so close to the train tracks I could've reached out and touched each car. That night, the train came by about once an hour. At least for that night, I learned an ultra-cheap night wasn't worth the money I was able to pocket.

Chapter 15: Situational Awareness

An important theme of this book is to remind you to be aware of your surroundings and continuously understand your options. As Susan likes to remind us, always look around and be situationally aware.

Does anyone look unusual as you walk among strangers? Is someone quickly walking towards you? What are people around you talking about? Is there a unique news story on the television? Is the building unusually empty or crowded? Are there more security guards than normal? Are those bomb-sniffing Border Patrol dogs or are the dogs just looking for illegal produce?

In today's world, life is solitary when your mind is buried in the screen of a mobile phone. Let's face it, we block out the external world all the time. Based on one study, millennials check their phones at least three hours daily.[25]

I get this. I too, spend a crazy amount of time on my mobile phone; however, when I'm traveling, life is different. I feel like time moves faster as I drop off my car at the airport, rush through security, check my email and texts repeatedly, and pick up some food and water for my trip all while racing to the gate in time to board. However, while I'm rushing around, and staring at my phone, I am constantly looking at my surroundings.

I have seen people walk away from their luggage in the middle of a crowded coffee shop. I have observed people fight over parking spaces. I know when the desk agent is about to call for standby passengers, and I can almost predict the cancellation of a flight. After decades of traveling, I feel I have developed a sixth sense in regards to trouble headed my way. Fortunately, I am now very good at anticipating problems and navigating my way to a safe and acceptable solution.

Situational awareness is accomplished by being cognizant of one's surroundings. Sure, my head is buried in my mobile as

---

[25] Kelly, Rhea, "Study: Millennials Spend More than Three Hours a Day on Mobile Phones, Campus Technology, November 19, 2015

much as everyone else, but I am constantly reminding myself to be alert, look around, and have a backup plan.

Always have a backup plan! Always have a plan B, and a plan C, and if necessary, a plan D. Unfortunately, except maybe in spy school, the skill of situational awareness is not taught. Yet, this skill can be developed through experience which means start looking at your surroundings. The more you are aware of your surroundings, the people, the social climate, the weather pattern, the security, the news, the flight schedules, the financial markets, the more resilient you will become.

A good example: it's late at night, you're at the airport, and the flight gets cancelled. Sometimes the airline will put you up in a hotel and other times you're on your own. If you're traveling for business, in most cases your employer will pay for your hotel room because remember, they want you safe and productive.

In the "it's late at night and my flight was cancelled" situation, I'm quickly accessing my "go to" hotel apps to understand my options. If my default, company-approved hotels are booked, and my company travel agent isn't helpful, then my plan C is **HotelTonight.**

A great app for last minute hotel rooms, HotelTonight displays local hotels with bargain last minute rates. While not all area hotels are included in the HotelTonight program, this app provides an easy mechanism to find hotels close to the airport and typically at a great rate.

The next two travel stories help illustrate the concept of situational awareness. The first story outlines what happened to many U.S. business travelers on September 11, 2001. Hundreds of thousands of people were stranded that day, but some lucky people made it home. The second story is a personal travel story told by my son who was returning home to the U.S. after backpacking in Europe. While not a business travel story, I think it's an important example of the randomness of travel challenges. The story demonstrates how patience and being aware of your surroundings can get you through unexpected obstacles.

Travel Story: I Need a Car, Courtesy of Andrew Burger, Florida

Tuesday, September 11, 2001, started off like most travel Tuesdays. I had an early flight to somewhere with a connection in Atlanta. During approach, our pilot announced all flights were asked to take a holding pattern. A few minutes later, the pilot announced we were ordered to land immediately. I was sitting up front, so I disembarked quickly when we arrived at the gate, and walked quickly to the Delta Crown Room (now called the Delta SkyClub) to find out what was going on and check on my connection.

As I watched television, I learned of an aircraft hitting the World Trade Center in New York City, and then I witnessed the second aircraft hitting the second tower. I instantly felt we were under attack.

First, I called my family in Miami Beach. I told them I was okay, and I would return home as quickly as possible.

Second, I called the toll-free numbers of multiple rental car companies, but the lines were all busy. Next, I called my company's travel department; fortunately, they were able to book me a car. (Remember, there were no mobile internet apps in those days.)

When I arrived to the National car rental lot, the customer line wrapped around the building, and everyone wanted a car to leave town. I skipped the line, walked up to the members' desk and said, "I have a reservation."

Within minutes I was in a minivan headed south on I-75 to Miami where I listened to news stations the entire ride.

Twelve-hours later, I was home in my crying wife's arms.

Meanwhile, my father was at a tradeshow in Las Vegas where he was stranded for over a week.

Travel Story: Bomb Shelter, Courtesy of Nathan Puldy, Washington

In the summer of 2014, I backpacked throughout Europe. Avoiding any serious trouble, I started my long journey home on an inexpensive, but complex flight plan: Dublin to London to Tel Aviv to Los Angeles to Denver.

Unknown to me, upon route from London to Tel Aviv, the FAA shut down all travel between Israel and the U.S. because rockets were being shot from Gaza towards Tel Aviv's Ben-Gurion Airport. Upon landing, my phone exploded with messages from friends and family. Turned out, my flight was one of the last foreign flights permitted to land in Israel.

I exited the plane anxious to see if my U.S.-bound flight would be allowed to depart. Before boarding my next flight, I needed to collect my bag outside of immigration, check-in at another airline, and then enter the departure hall. As I made my way through the airport, I passed numerous "bomb shelter" signs, which slightly raised my anxiety.

At immigration, I was interrogated by airport security. They acted as if everything I told them was a lie, and after my first round of questioning, they sent me to their supervisor. I experienced a second round of questions before I was allowed to collect my bag.

Arriving at the check-in desk, my bag was declared too heavy, and I was forced to repack. While repacking, sirens started screaming, and I saw everyone rushing past the check-in desks, deeper into the airport, toward bomb shelters. The Israeli airport employees who helped me check-in were laughing with each other.

At that point, I realized the sirens and the air raid were not a big deal. This wasn't their first rodeo, and I told myself, if the locals aren't worried then I shouldn't either.

We all walked toward the bomb shelter and hung out for roughly twenty minutes before the sirens stopped and Israeli life returned to their normal. I finished check-in, and entered the security checkpoint where I was selected for an additional screening. Again, I emptied my bags. Meanwhile, the airline employees were going through their pre-flight procedures as if there was no danger.

Eventually, I boarded the plane; soon, I was in the air, and safely headed back home to the U.S.

Chapter 16: Closing Comments

Traveling for business can be one of the most exciting moments of your business career, but it can be the most miserable too.

Don't let the uncertainty and the challenges of business travel deter you from reaching your business goals. Traveling is one of the fastest ways to expand your career because of the endless opportunities to grow your mind and your cultural understanding of the people in this world.

Knowing how to travel, where to go, what to say, what not to say, when to relax, and when to be aggressive, makes all the difference in becoming a successful and savvy road warrior. Traveling from point A to point B has also never been easier with the plethora of smartphone options combined with travel apps; consequently, today's high-tech road warrior is better equipped than ever to navigate the world of business travel.

Along the way, you will discover new travel challenges and your own secret tips to tour the world. As you grow your miles rewards programs, and your knowledge of amazing hotels and restaurants, from time to time, please take pause and share some of your travel secrets with the next generation of travelers.

But for now, jump in and experience the thrill of a business trip.

Appendix: More Travel Stories

The best parts of travel are the stories. But let's be specific: the best stories are the travel horror stories or the "no way did that happen" kind of story. Here are some selected tales I think you'll enjoy.

Michael Puldy, California

The TSA Inspection

In the days before TSA Precheck, I was going through security at John Wayne's Orange County airport and running late. For whatever reason, I was pulled from the line and they ran a chemical scan on my bags and on me. Surprisingly, my bags turned up positive for chemicals that could have been used in explosives.

This was bad.

I was pulled aside and taken to a private area where security searched me thoroughly and emptied all the contents of my bags. They asked me lots of personal questions as well as my reasons for being in Orange County.

When they found nothing, they told me why they pulled me aside and put me through interrogation. In short, they concluded the rental car must have been used to transport fertilizer, and the chemical compounds from the fertilizer rubbed off on my carry-on luggage when it was in the trunk of the car. During the scrub of my luggage, the machines picked up the chemical traces and this set TSA into alert mode.

Racing to London Heathrow

I was driving the rental car back to London Heathrow from our assignment in Hursley near Southampton. Only an hour's drive, we left early with plenty of time to make our 10:00 a.m. flight back to the U.S.

The local roads of the UK were twisty and narrow as I drove through one small town after another - plus driving too fast on the left side of the road in a right wheel car added some additional degree of difficulty. I could feel the left side wheels of the car hit the curb on more than one occasion, and then I hit the curb too hard and blew out a tire.

Changing a flat on a rental car was not too much fun, but it was nice to have two people to help me. We changed the flat in fifteen minutes, and I drove a little slower to the airport.

Upon arrival at the rental return, I casually mentioned I had a flat tire, we changed the tire, and that the flat was in the back. After healthy discussion, I was told I had to settle the issue inside at the counter.

After more debate, I was charged $100 for the flat tire, and the three of us left to catch our flight.

The Jakarta Hai-Lai Club

My colleague and I were in Jakarta, Indonesia, for two days of discussions with one of the country's leading banks. As customary for these types of meetings, we were invited to dinner. Our hosts said we were going to a place called The Jai-Alai Club.

I was excited and surprised Jai-Alai was a game played in Indonesia. Jai-Alai is a game of Basque origin that was played in South Florida, and I was trying to figure out how this sport made it to the other side of the world.

When we arrived, it was clear this was a different kind of Jai-Alai. For starters, the sign on the building was spelled differently.

The Hai-Lai club in Jakarta was combination Las Vegas style nightclub and karaoke bar. We entered through the basement where we walked past a series of karaoke rooms with frosted glass. Taking the stairs to the main floor, our group of a dozen people, all in suits, entered a giant ballroom filled with people where a singer pranced around the stage singing songs in a language I didn't recognize.

Around 10:00 p.m., the families left, but the men stayed. There were hundreds of people in this grand ballroom. Our host escorted us to the back where dozens of women were waiting all dressed up with numbers on their dresses. Some mingled with the guests, while others sat on bleachers behind frosted glass. The glass had a thin clear strip so we could look at the women, but they couldn't see us.

When we figured out what was going on, we politely declined the offer to participate. "So sorry," we were told, "our host has already paid. Besides, these ladies are just for conversation."

It was a strange experience. After some discussion, we decided we would follow the lead of our host; after all, we could maintain decorum by only engaging in conversation.

Within minutes, two ladies came over and sat with us for the next hour and a half. Since they barely spoke English, we didn't have a lot to talk about. At midnight, the evening was over, we were respectful to our company, and we safely and happily returned to our hotel for drinks and laughter about our crazy evening.

Drinks at the JW Marriott Hotel at Tomorrow Square

The JW Marriott Hotel Tomorrow Square in Shanghai, China, is one of the most beautiful hotels I've ever visited. The building is an architectural marvel, and overlooks Tomorrow Square, a beautiful park in Shanghai.

For my visit, I was upgraded to a corner room near the very top floor of the hotel. I was on floor fifty-eight, and down the hall was the Chairman's Suite. The executive lounge was one floor up, and offered amazing panoramic views of the city of Shanghai.

Since I was staying on the top floor of the hotel, I figured I was permitted to use the lounge accessible by staircase near my room.

Sitting on a couch, the views of the nighttime traffic and the lights of Shanghai were truly breathtaking, and one of the most memorable moments of peace and happiness during all of my business travels. There I was sitting on the couch, deep in thought, drinking a wonderful single malt scotch, when the host came over and said, "Mr. Puldy, I'm sorry, but your room does not include the benefits of the executive lounge. Please kindly pay for your drink, and you can leave when you are finished."

Boom! He really burst my tranquility balloon. At least the lounge host was nice about asking me to leave.

Chicken Feet

Lunchtime in Jakarta. In Asia, most meals are served at round tables where the food is placed on a rotating wheel, or "Lazy Susan." My colleague and I were with our Indonesian hosts, and they were ordering our lunch.

Somewhere in the middle of the meal, our server brought a plate of fried chicken feet.

Until this moment, I only saw chicken feet on living chickens, so this was a little bit of a shock. Our hosts turned the Lazy Susan so the food was closest to us, and requested that we try the chicken feet first. Everyone at the table was smiling to see how we would react when someone asked us, "Have you ever tried chicken feet before?"

In my mind, I'm thinking this is a rhetorical question, and they must be playing with our heads.

I took my chopsticks and reached in to grab a piece of chicken. My colleague did the same. I remember the chicken feet being chewy and probably more ligament and bone than meat.

Our hosts smiled broadly at our bravery and everyone laughed.

No Credit Cards

Eating at picnic tables in a very local restaurant in Frankfurt, the English menu said "no credit cards." I asked the waitress if they were serious, and if they took credit cards. She said, "yes" in English! When the time came to pay the bill, I found out the waitress was wrong, and I needed German currency. Fortunately, during my dinner, I was befriended by a U.S. flight crew eating next to me. A pilot bought my dinner, and I mailed him a check covering his expenses when I returned to the U.S. I was lucky.

Traveling to PEK via TUS, LAX, SFO, HKG, PVG, and TSN

My flight from Tucson to Los Angeles started on time, but the leg from LAX to San Francisco was delayed. I arrived in SFO just eleven minutes before the departure of my connecting flight to Beijing. An airline concierge met me upon arrival and redirected me to a different flight, headed to Hong Kong, where I would then connect to a Beijing flight.

Almost fifteen hours later, I arrived in Hong Kong to discover my flight to Beijing was canceled; however, my U.S.-based airline carrier said my best option was to fly to Shanghai and then take a national carrier, China Eastern, to Beijing.

Since this was the era before e-tickets, the only way to travel was with a printed ticket. Some tickets were transferrable between airlines while others were not. In this case, the agent in Hong Kong told me I would need a new ticket issued by China Eastern, and I could collect this ticket once I arrived in Shanghai.

On to Shanghai. After three-hours of flying and some difficulty navigating the airport, I found an agent who spoke enough English to print my Beijing ticket.

My flight to Beijing was scheduled to depart at 10:00 p.m. local time, and I would arrive around midnight. Since my Beijing hotel was sending a car, while in Hong Kong, I left a message for my hotel that I was arriving much later than planned and gave them my best guess on arrival.

Naturally, as we approached Beijing Capital Airport, the airplane was diverted due to fog. As we were landing at a strange and nameless airport, I'm thinking I will rent a car and drive to Beijing; however, that was the jet lag and the fatigue talking. Who was I kidding? I had no idea where I was, how to rent a car or where I was going. There was no such thing as Google Maps, and I didn't even have a quality map of China.

When we landed, and the plane was parked on the tarmac, I noticed multiple planes landed in succession behind us. All the planes scheduled for landing in Beijing were being rerouted to this place somewhere in China.

There were only two westerners sitting in first class: a man across the aisle and myself. He looked at me and asked if I knew what was going on. I said, "not really," and he proceeded to tell me. He was an expat living in China, formerly from the UK, and he spoke fluent Mandarin.

This is when I found out we were diverted to a city to the south called Tianjin about 100 miles from Beijing, and here we would stay, inside the plane until the fog cleared.

The airport ramp crew drove portable airplane stairs to our plane, and we sat with the main door open for a few hours. There were a dozen other planes also on the tarmac as we all sat in a nice row waiting for the Beijing fog to lift.

About three plus hours later, our flight taxied down a Tianjin runway, and we landed in Beijing close to 4:00 a.m. Thank goodness I didn't check a bag that trip because my luggage would have never caught up with me.

Upon arrival in Beijing, to my shock, the hotel driver was waiting.

Room Occupied

As a postscript to my crazy flight to Beijing, the hotel experience was equally bizarre.

My driver dropped me off at the hotel close to 5:00 a.m. local time. My business breakfast was at 10:00 a.m. Upon check-in, I asked the receptionist if they had any upgrades available with a larger bed. After looking at a number of paper printouts, she said the hotel was sold out.

She asked if I needed help finding my room. With my one bag, I typically would have said no thank you, but I was so tired at this point I didn't care. As the bellman led me to my average room, all I could think of was sleep. I was so exhausted.

The bellman took my key and opened the door to the room. Sure enough, there was someone in my room! All I could see was a pair of legs wearing pants and socks, and a piece of open luggage near the foot of the bed. It was like this guy opened his suitcase, took off his shoes, and passed out.

The bellman was stunned and very apologetic. I was barely moved by the scene; however, I was happy he was a witness, and I didn't have to go downstairs and explain it to reception.

The two of us went back to reception, and within a few minutes, the desk clerk found another room in their "sold out" hotel. This time the bellman escorted me to my upgraded, larger room, on a nicer floor.

Changing Clothes Upon Approach

I slept fantastic in my coach seat during my eight-hour flight from Washington Dulles to Frankfurt. The problem was, I slept too good! I woke up as we were on approach, and in my haze I was admiring the patchwork grasses of Germany when I realized I was still in my green medical scrubs and a red sweatshirt. We were still around ten minutes from touchdown and my real clothes were in the overhead bin.

Too late to go to the lavatory, I was able to retrieve my street clothes from my luggage inside the overhead bin. Sitting back down I pulled the blanket over me and proceeded to take off my scrubs and put on my jeans. I then replaced my sweatshirt with a real shirt plus socks and shoes, as our plane hit the runway.

Although I observed some strange looks from my seatmates, by the time we were parked at the gate I was fully dressed and ready to disembark.

My Missing Rental Car

I hear countless stories of people losing their laptop in their valet parked rental car.

One night I attended a business dinner in Mahwah, New Jersey. We had a great client dinner, and my colleagues and I closed down the restaurant. When the valet brought me a white Ford Fiesta, it sure looked like my car, but it wasn't. Apparently, the valet gave *my* white Ford Fiesta to someone who was too drunk to notice the difference. Inside this car, we found his mobile phone, his laptop, and lots of other fun things. We even called his wife from his mobile phone to ask where he was staying. She had no clue.

The cops eventually tracked him down around 3:00 a.m. where he was passed out in his hotel room. For some reason when I was dropping off the car, at the last minute, I decided to take my laptop bag inside to dinner. While I was inconvenienced, it could have been a lot worse.

The Honor of Eating a Fish Head

In the late 90s, I made my first trip to Singapore.

My hosts took me to dinner at a seafood restaurant near an area called East Coast Lagoon. We ate on the second floor of a small restaurant with a nice view of the Singapore Straits.

We ordered an array of seafood, including Sri Lankan Crab and a big fish.

After we plowed through all of the food, and what seemed like a case of Tiger beer, the only thing left to eat was the head of the fish. Since I was the guest, I had the right of first refusal. I laughed at my new friends, then we all laughed together. There was no way I was eating a fish head.

The three of them did something like draw lots, and the winner took his chopsticks and played with the fish head before lifting the jaws into his mouth. I looked at him in amazement as he chewed on the fleshy jaws. Within a minute, he pulled the jawbones with the fish teeth still attached out of his mouth and placed it neatly on the plate.

The guy next to him then plucked the eye out of the socket of the fish with his chopsticks and quickly ate it like a green pea. The third guy ate the other eye, and between the three of them quickly demolished the fish head.

No Undershirts

There was a time I always wore undershirts under my dress shirts, and going to a meeting without an undershirt just wasn't possible.

The year was around 2008, and I traveled on Sunday from Denver to San Jose. When I arrived at my hotel room, I realized

I forgot my undershirts. Unfortunately, I didn't have a car. So, after dinner, I borrowed my colleague's rental car and drove to Target. My problem was Target had closed, and the next option was a Walmart forty-five minutes away in Oakland.

There I was, at 10:00 p.m., on Sunday night, browsing in an Oakland Walmart looking for undershirts. I was surprised at how crowded Walmart was at such a late hour. When I paid, I noticed the cashier was wearing latex blue gloves. I had never seen this before and thought it was quite odd.

Today, I see more and more people handling money wearing protective gloves.

Steve Gilbert, Florida

Dressing for a Meeting

Dressing for a late morning meeting, I realized my pants were wrinkled from my travels. I pulled out the hotel room iron and ironing board from the closet and prepared to fix the problem. Upon placing the iron on my pants, the iron began to melt, destroying both my pants and the iron.

With no backup pair of pants, and with an hour to go until my client meeting, I frantically searched the internet for a local department store. Fortunately, I was able to find a store close by, and I quickly found a pair of pants that worked. I was in and out of the store in ten minutes, and arrived at my meeting right on time.

Susan Weiss, California

Shrink-Wrapped Luggage

I was traveling from New York's JFK to Marrakech via Madrid. JFK to MAD was American Airlines, and MAD to RAK was Iberia Airlines.

American couldn't check me, or my bag, all the way. This meant I needed to clear immigration in Madrid, collect my bag from AA baggage claim, recheck my bag with Iberia, collect a new boarding pass, and then clear Spain's immigration before boarding my flight to RAK.

Unfortunately, the flight out of JFK was delayed, and I landed in MAD thirty minutes before my connecting flight. To complicate my situation, upon arrival, I found out Iberia was in another terminal and there was no way I was going to make my connecting flight to Marrakech. Iberia rerouted me through Casablanca, and I spent fifteen hours in Madrid's airport waiting for my next flight. Along the way, I noticed many people shrink-wrapping their luggage. I thought these people were crazy, or they just bought cheap luggage.

My flight to Casablanca was delayed which meant I once again missed my connecting flight to Marrakech.

As my luggage rolled out of the conveyor belt in Casablanca, my bag was shredded on one side, and my clothes were hanging out of the bag.

Around noon, the next day, my now shrink-wrapped luggage and I arrived safely in Marrakech's Menara Airport.

Status Matters

Traveling from New York to South Africa via London, my London to South Africa flight was delayed due to equipment problems (code for airplane mechanical issues). American Airlines canceled the flight. Since the cancellation was mechanical, all passengers were awarded hotel and food vouchers for the inconvenience; however, we had to go to a specific service desk to claim them.

When I arrived, the line was ridiculously long. Since I was an American Platinum flying in business class, I was able to take advantage of the American Platinum desk. Instead of the crazy line, there were only three people ahead of me in the Platinum line, and I was headed to my hotel within ten minutes.

I'm positive I was checked into the hotel and having dinner by the time the last people from that first line got their vouchers.

Flying one airline with status has benefits.

Chris Pantano, New York

Penthouse Upgrade

During a trip to Newport Beach, I was staying at a high-end hotel for two nights with several colleagues. The day we were planning to check out, we found out we needed to stay one more night so before leaving for our meetings, we told the front desk to extend our rooms. The hotel was booked and they struggled with our request, but eventually made it work.

Upon returning to the hotel late that evening, I entered my room to discover someone else was there! The two of us were both surprised, but he was very nice about the situation and allowed me to look for my clothes and my suitcase. Both were gone.

It was near midnight, and the clerk at the front desk had no idea what was going on. Soon, the night manager was involved and he offered me a drink in the lounge while they figured out their next steps. While waiting, I called my colleagues to see if they had a similar problem, but they were all fine in their original rooms. My colleagues elected to join me in the lounge where we went a little crazy. For the next few hours, we ordered shots, hors d'oeuvres, top shelf drinks, and added a nice tip for the waiter.

Around 2:00 a.m., the night manager found me, apologized for the confusion, and escorted me to the Penthouse room where I was reunited with my clothes. My new accommodations had a private balcony, a telescope, multiple couches, extra nice bathrobes, and a fully stocked fridge complete with full size snacks and drinks.

The next morning at check out, I was handed a $225 bar bill. The front desk said only one drink was on the house. I expressed my frustration with the hotel overall and threatened to contact the corporate office and detail the entire charade.

I never had to pay the bar tab.

Brandi Boatner, New York

First Class Kiosk

I arrived at JFK for my flight to Barcelona. This was my first international business trip, and I was excited and anxious when I checked-in at the airline kiosk.

As I went through the check-in process, there were a number of prompts for me to scroll through. One of the prompts asked if I wanted to upgrade my coach seat for $100. Now, the flight was six hours long, and the way the question was worded I thought it was mandatory for me to say, "Yes." Without thinking too much, I quickly selected the upgrade and paid the additional fare.

Of course, even though business class was a great experience, I admit I felt funny. Being of a millennial mindset, and with only one year in my job, I felt somewhat out of place. It may be customary for executives to fly business class, but not for me. Anyway, the experience was fun.

I didn't think much of it until I returned home and completed my expense report. Unfortunately, my expense report was rejected. Only then did I learn my business class upgrade was out of policy, and I wouldn't be reimbursed.

William Hahn, California
(Travel Stories from the 1960s)

LA to Paris

I departed around 10:30 p.m. on a nonstop flight from Los Angeles to Paris. Seated to my right in first class was an attractive, middle-aged woman.

As we taxied for takeoff, she looked out the window and sobbed quietly. We were barely airborne when she turned to me and placed her head on my shoulder; I placed my arms around her and her tears wet my shirt. No words were exchanged, and we fell into a light sleep in each other's arms.

The next morning, during a meal prior to landing in Paris, we engaged in pleasant conversation and made no mention of the doings of the night before.

International Tipping

On my first visit to Bangkok, it was late when I arrived at the Intercontinental Hotel. I was escorted to my room by a valet who brought my luggage. As he was leaving, I gave him a tip. Suddenly, he began to fuss over me, helping me with my jacket, opening my suitcase, and once again checking the room. It seemed like a long time before he finally left.

Later, I learned the tip I gave him was almost a week's salary.

Pat Corcoran, New York

Taking an Unregistered Taxi

My first trip to South Korea lasted twenty-plus hours across two flights, and I landed in Seoul around 4:30 a.m. My colleagues already arrived, and they gave me an estimate of the taxi fare from the airport to the hotel.

I converted U.S. dollars into South Korean Won at a previous airport, and I thought I had enough for the journey to the hotel. I was exhausted from jet lag, so when I was offered a ride, I asked how much. One guy offered what seemed like a low number so I accepted.

As I stepped inside his van, I felt I had made a mistake: no meter and no taxi disclaimers. Next, the driver asked me to talk to someone on the phone who could speak English about the hotel address and the price. Another red flag. Regardless, I did a currency conversion on my phone and realized I did not have enough money.

I told the driver, and the person on the phone, I didn't have enough cash, and I needed to go inside the hotel to secure more money. About 45 minutes later, I was excited to see my hotel in the distance, but my excitement quickly changed as the driver drove past the hotel. Now I was worried.

I had no idea where he was taking me. A few minutes later, the driver stopped at a 7-Eleven and said, "ATM." He pointed inside. I knew how much local currency I needed to pay the taxi, so I went inside the store, but the ATM was out of order. The driver then drove me to another 7-Eleven. We went inside. The driver hovered behind me, and I had to motion him to back away from me and the ATM machine. He looked anxious.

This time the ATM machine worked, and the driver required me to pay him before he would take me to my hotel.

When I told the hotel receptionist what I paid, the receptionist said I had paid nearly three times the standard rate.

My International Roaming Phone

Prior to traveling to the Philippines, I contacted my mobile phone provider to make sure I had international coverage, and that my phone, both calls and data, would work in the Philippines. My carrier told me yes to both.

I landed in Manila, and went directly to my hotel to unpack, eat dinner and then to bed. Around noon the next day, I received a text message on my mobile phone that I had exceeded the data limit.

I incurred over $1,200 in charges.

I thought the data portion of my phone was shut off so I didn't understand how my bill could run up like that overnight.

With a twelve-hour time difference, it was a struggle communicating with my mobile phone carrier back in the U.S. Eventually, I connected to someone who understood the problem, and I was told I was misinformed when they originally told me that my data plan would work in the Philippines. The client service representative apologized, but could do nothing until the end of the month - two weeks away! I screamed, I yelled, I pleaded, but no success.

The data portion of my phone (e.g., maps and apps) was useless the rest of my trip.

Susan Schreitmueller, Texas

The Importance of Being "Situationally Aware"

A colleague was traveling with me in a foreign country. As a typical "sales guy," he was *always* on his phone. One day, he was outside a hotel gate and paying far more attention to his phone than who was coming upon him.

Unfortunately, he was accosted and hurt quite seriously because he didn't remain situationally aware.

Michael Errity, Georgia

The World's Best Peanut Butter and Jelly Sandwich

Riding a packed parking lot shuttle bus into Atlanta Airport, I was famished after a long day without a meal. I opened my briefcase to find two peanut butter and jelly sandwiches. A fellow passenger remarked that the sandwiches looked like a great treat, and I immediately offered to share one of my sandwiches.

Apparently, many passengers watched my act of kindness because the people on the bus repetitively made comments like, "I wish I had a PB&J in my briefcase," and "That looks like the perfect PB&J." Next, the bus driver said she had not had time for lunch, and she wished she had a PB&J.

Without a word, in a moment of inspired southern hospitality, I handed the bus driver my second PB&J asking her to promise she would enjoy it. The crowd loved it, and there was spontaneous applause from my fellow riders.

Later that night, my wife and daughter phoned me from home, and said they were listening to the radio and randomly reached "The Delilah" program, where people call in and make a dedication.

Here's what they heard: "I'm a bus driver at the Atlanta airport, and I'd like to dedicate this song to the gentleman who generously shared with me the best peanut butter and jelly sandwich ever made."

Brad Donaldson, Georgia

Lost in Translation

Arriving in Spain, I was completely drained. We proceeded to spend the day working while my coworker taught me as much Spanish as possible which wasn't much. I crashed that night, never bolted the door, and in the morning the maid knocked, and hearing no reply, she entered my room.

I was in a comatose state where I could hear her knock and hear the door open, but I was under the bed covers and unable to talk or move. I kept fighting the jet lag and tried to wake up when, just as she walked to the end of the bed, I sprung up and yelled out the only Spanish that came to my head, "Las luces!" (the lights!). The poor lady jumped into the air like a deer and sprinted to the door. I am sure she thought I was the biggest jerk in the hotel.

The Hotel Bar

As a recent college graduate, I was on my first big international trip. After a long flight from the U.S. to Hong Kong, I checked into my five star hotel and went to the bar to grab a beer. I was surprised how nice the people were as the woman next to me immediately made conversation. I asked her where she lived, and she replied Hong Kong.

Puzzled, I asked, "Why come to a hotel bar if you live here?"

She looked at me like I was a complete idiot and turned to the guy on her other side.

Michele Kochoff Platt, Alabama

Happy Birthday from Athens

After a night with a colleague that involved dinner and Greek "Retsina" (pine resin wine), I settled inside my room at the downtown Athens Hilton. About midnight, I received a call from my dinner colleague who asked me, "Where are you sleeping tonight?"

Of course, I was speechless. After a very uncomfortable five seconds, I said, "Right here!" and hung up the phone.

Totally enraged, and ignoring the seven-hour time zone difference, I called my wise friend in Orlando, who talked me down from enraged to pity.

After both calls, I was totally awake and wondering who could I call next. Aha! It's November 21, and the birthday of a new business friend, Don Platt, then living in St Louis. So I placed a surprise call to Don, and wished him happy birthday from Athens!

We had a great conversation, and then I got ready for bed. To my surprise, Don called me back with an invitation to celebrate New Year's Eve in St. Louis.

We were married six months later.

Erich Elit, Colorado

Change of Plans

In 1987, I was traveling the world performing emergency support services on mainframe computers. I was twenty-three years old, but was quickly becoming a seasoned traveler. I was on assignment in London for two weeks, and when I returned to my Minneapolis apartment, the answering machine light was blinking. Back then, office phones, payphones and voicemail were the only ways to communicate. Email was also limited.

The message played, "Erich, I hope you had a good trip. We need you to go to Hong Kong tomorrow. Call me as soon as you get this."

After washing some loads of laundry and a short night's sleep in my own bed, I was off to Hong Kong.

The flight plan was Minneapolis to San Francisco to Narita, Japan and then to Hong Kong. As planned, the trip was scheduled to take about twenty-four hours. Unfortunately, traveling rarely goes as planned. The flight from Japan to Hong Kong had mechanical issues, and the gate agent told us the flight would be canceled. Then, at the last minute, as many of us started to make other arrangements, the plane was ready to go and the flight was reinstated.

I arrived late in Hong Kong.

Typically, when I arrive at an airport, my driver would be waiting for me holding a sign with my name. This trip was no different, and my driver was supposed to meet me at the airport, but when I arrived there was no driver. It was about 11:00 p.m., the airport was packed with people, and I was jet lagged.

Since this was the day before mobile phones, my backup plan was an office phone number, but the payphones in the airport were completely foreign. Luckily, I was able to solicit the help of an English-speaking teenaged girl, and she helped me place a call to the office. Unfortunately, at such a late hour, all I could do was leave a voicemail.

At this point, I needed to find a place to sleep and sort things out, so I went outside the airport to look for a hotel. As it turned out, there was another guy from my flight who had the same problem, and we both walked over to the airport hotel to inquire about rooms. Believe it or not, the hotel only had one room, and while I'm not sure how smart this was, the other guy and I decided to share the last remaining room.

In the end, the trip all worked out, and I connected with my people in the morning.

Michael Goldman, Georgia

Lost Luggage

One of my worst trips was to Sarnia, Ontario, Canada, to inspect a chemical spill cleanup. The trip was in January, and I knew it would be cold. I packed my warmest clothes and boarded the plane in jeans and a denim jacket. Delta lost my luggage, and I arrived in Ontario where the temperature was thirty degrees below zero Fahrenheit.

Delta assured me that my bags would be delivered to the hotel. I hit the field the next morning in my jean jacket. I had no idea how cold I would be, and at every opportunity, I ran back inside a building. Needless to say, my trips outside were shorter and shorter, and I kept my spirits up knowing my winter gear would be waiting for me at my hotel.

It wasn't.

Another call. Delta assured me the bags were on their way, and I would not have to buy another coat and lined pants. The next day was colder than the first, and oddly enough, I was so cold I began to sweat. I returned to the hotel, but still no bags.

Another phone call, more assurance, but no bag.

I put my wet and cold clothes on the radiator to dry, and within seconds the hotel room smelled like my feet and butt crack. This lasted for a week.

My bags never turned up.

To this day, I leave home dressed for my destination.

Stephen Puldy, Florida

Travels in China During the Early 1980s

During the early 1980's, when I first traveled to China, things were very different from today. Most of all, it was not easy to do business in China. A company needed an invitation or connection just to visit. Making life more complicated, the only airlines flying from Hong Kong to mainland China were owned and operated by the Chinese government. These planes were usually Russian or older 1950's vintage U.S. aircraft.

One of the practices followed by the native Chinese passengers when flying was to leave their seats and move to the front of the plane as soon as the announcement came that the flight was in its final approach. Nothing the flight attendants could say or do would keep the Chinese passengers in their seats in the rush to be the first off the flight. It was also common practice to carry large amounts of luggage and other personal items on board. Even though I never personally saw this, I did hear tales of people carrying live animals on flights such as chickens in cages.

Checking into a flight in China could also be time consuming. There were always two lines, one for Chinese natives and one for foreigners. Of course, there was usually only one or two attendants to check you in. The Chinese passengers received priority, and foreigners had to wait until an attendant could "find time" to deal with us.

On one trip flying domestically inside China, our flight was delayed. Everyone on the flight was in a room waiting for the plane to arrive when an announcement was made that lunch would be served due to the delay. The citizens rushed to the food line, picked up a bowl and received a bowl of hot broth. I joined the back of the line and tried the soup; needless to say, not my best lunch.

China had two types of currency: one for Chinese citizens, and one for foreigners; furthermore, changing currency on the black market was quite common. There were also stores in China that sold goods exclusively to foreigners. Even though foreigners could shop anywhere, it was against the law for Chinese citizens to buy at stores designated "foreigner only."

I remember one time being in a store looking for a souvenir and being surrounded by about a dozen Chinese just watching me shop. At the time, it was a novelty to see a foreigner in China.

Regarding hotels, locals operated the best hotels in China since many international chains had not yet arrived. The rooms had the barest of furnishings. I remember the television was black and white with maybe a twelve-inch screen, and since the government controlled the programs, there were only one or two channels. Television options were extremely limited composed of local news in Chinese and old American westerns; moreover, "the broadcast day" was only several hours long.

Since there were few choices to eat when in a Chinese city, we usually had to take our meals in the hotel, and it was some of the worse food I have ever eaten. Once I ordered a Coca-Cola thinking since it was served in a bottle, and because the bottle looked like a Coca-Cola, it would be all right to drink. Much to my disappointment, the colored drink was not a Coke, but only flavored water inside a Coca-Cola bottle.

Finally, when I was visiting Hong Kong, I took a train ride to Canton (now called Guangzhou). At the time, foreigners could only schedule a day trip and were required to return to Hong Kong by that evening. There was no staying over in a Chinese city. Anyway, everywhere I looked, there were signs on the train stating, "no smoking," but most of the Chinese smoked all of the time and nothing was said.

About the Author

Michael Puldy (michael@nextgentraveler.com) is a technology executive, photographer, writer and world traveler. Between travels for business and pleasure, he has visited over forty countries and the continents of Africa, Asia, Australia, Europe, North America and South America.

A Florida native and resident for almost thirty-five years, Michael left Florida only two times before attending college at Clemson University in Clemson, South Carolina. During his freshman year, Michael experienced the joy of road trips driving throughout the South, the Northeast and the Midwest. He also lived his first college summer near the District of Columbia. The next year, the summer between Michael's sophomore and junior years, he backpacked in the Middle East and North Africa followed by traveling solo in Western Europe and the United Kingdom. These early life adventures fostered his love of travel, meeting people and experiencing different cultures, religions, and customs.

Michael has visited all fifty United States, and has lived in Arizona, Colorado, Florida, Maryland, Massachusetts, South Carolina and Singapore. He now resides in Los Angeles, California with his wife Adrienne, and Boomer, their Yorkshire terrier.

A member of the Circumnavigators Club, his travel highlights include: trekking to Mount Everest Base Camp in Nepal, sailing to observe the Komodo Dragons in Indonesia, living on a dive boat exploring the Great Barrier Reef in Australia, backpacking in Denali and Lake Clark National Parks in Alaska, white water rafting down the Colorado River and hiking the Grand Canyon, watching the sunrise in Yosemite near Half Dome, touring the Valley of the Kings and the Step Pyramid in Egypt, becoming engaged at the base of Mount Fitz Roy near El

Chalten, Argentina, and meeting the most amazing and incredible people all across the globe.

Professionally, Michael has spent his entire career in the technology industry where he has worked in the aerospace, financial, retail and technology sectors. He is also a published author of professional and peer reviewed papers. In addition, he has held three global jobs based in the U.S., and lived two years as an expatriate in Singapore.

Photos from Michael's selected travels throughout the world can be viewed at www.puldy.com. You can also follow his Instagram (www.instagram.com/mpuldy) and Twitter feed (www.twitter.com/NextGen_Travelr).

Made in the USA
San Bernardino, CA
07 December 2016